6
6

COVER ART: Jacques Kleynhans.

INTERIOR ILLUSTRATIONS: Antoine Cossé.

Printed in the United States.

Anna Akhmatova translations by Katie Farris and Ilya Kaminsky

DEAR MCSWEENEY'S,

I inherited a hand-me-down electric breast pump from my friend Jenny. I'd wager I'm not the only new mother who heard her breast pump talking to her. In the machine's whirl—a tight system that relies on boob suction to create a vacuum—the motor spoke to me. It said, "Meat tower," over and over again. Robotically. "Meat tower. Meat tower. Meat tower," while I harvested four to eight ounces of breast milk from my body. I'd picture a skyscraper-sized hunk of gyro meat roasting on a stick, or a mile-high pile of thinly sliced prosciutto, a pastrami sandwich from Katz's. A meat tower. Was I the tower of meat my borrowed breast pump referred to? The inventor Nikola Tesla called humans meat machines, and certainly I'd never felt this assessment to be more accurate than during the period of my life when my body made food to feed three other humans.

Why, of all the messages the ghost in this machine might have to relate, was "meat tower" the one I heard? How is "meat tower" different from the message in your breast pump? Or the words your elderly dishwasher says to you each night after supper?

The ghosts in my machines speak a lot because I have an affinity for aged devices. I don't really like new things. Waste is a design flaw, and capitalism is a sick system. I don't like to make trash. I had a college crush on a man who produced only one small paper bag of garbage over an entire year. I thought that was extremely sexy. Old things are usually made better and more interesting, even if some of the machines in my life suffer from dementia or hearing loss. I have an EarthLink email account, got it in the '90s. It delivers about 90 percent of my emails. It's like the pony express of emails. It's exciting. Will my messages make it through? Maybe. Maybe not. My email address practices the Japanese principle of wabi-sabi, an aesthetic that finds beauty in the imperfect, impermanent, and incomplete. People tease me about my email address and I think, Oh, you poor follower of the new, surfer of trends.

My phone is ancient; my laptop is old; my car is geriatric. I hate putting tools out to pasture when they still have usefulness. My daughters are embarrassed to arrive at school in our old jalopy. They groan when I tell them the real shame is people who buy new cars before they've used up the ones they already own. They can't believe I still wear clothes I owned in high school. But I hate

our disposable way of life. Plus,
I respect a device that acknowl-
edges its mortality, shows its age.
Faulty devices are porous and
allow space enough for difference
and different outcomes. They are
anti-bureaucracy. In that way,
I think aged devices can help us be
anti-fascist, too, can help us stay
open and nonjudgmental as they
remind us that the only certainty is
the cycle of decay.

My dad smoked cigarettes most
of his life. He carried with him
little packages of death, memento
mori. He kept his smokes close,
as if they were his dearest friends,
until those cigarettes finally did
what they had always promised
they would do: they murdered
him. People do have to die.
I understand that. In what way do
you keep death and decay present?
A rotting tree? A rotting tooth?
A torn shirt? A broken machine?
A broken mind?

Thomas Edison tried to invent
an electronic megaphone for talking
to the dead. I wish I had one. With
all these older tools and devices
around, maybe I do. Maybe it's
just a little bit broken, and in that
brokenness the dead, or at least the
death inside us, is able to speak.

Love,

SAMANTHA HUNT
TIVOLI, NEW YORK

DEAR MCSWEENEY'S,
This letter is about a lie I told in
middle school that I am still living
in the shadow of almost twenty
years later.

Like millions of deeply
repressed Black girls, I grew up
in the church. More specifically,
I grew up a budding Pentecostal
in an Assemblies of God church
in Englewood, New Jersey. The
church no longer exists (it was
dismantled because of a coup
against the standing pastor, after
embezzlement charges were lev-
eled against him to throw off the
scent of looting board members,
so that should tell you everything
you need to know). Most of my
childhood years were spent in
that church. We celebrated Fall
Festival instead of Halloween
because kids still wanted a reason
to dress up and eat candy, and
parents didn't want to hear their
kids complain about missing out
on the devil's holiday. We had
Missionettes and Royal Rangers,
which was like the Girl and Boy
Scouts but with significantly more
Jesus and literally no cookies.
We had Turkey Football games,
and mission trips to Mexico, and
Fine Arts Festivals, and all these
activities made my twelve-year-old
self think, This Christian thing
is doable. And I lived for Youth

Group every Friday. I was a social child and had plenty of friends at school, but my Youth Group friends were the ones I didn't have to hide from my mom. Every service started with a few worship songs (always led by the hottest kids at church), then continued on to the sermon (from Pastor Josh, an actor turned pastor who always reminded us that he almost beat out Christian Bale for the role of Batman), and closed out with more worship and an altar call (which tended to include a spiritual breakthrough or two). After the official service was done, the kids would go downstairs to hang out, flirt with the worship team members, and eat pounds of Mama Teresa's famous mac and cheese. This was how it normally went.

One Friday night after worship, I went up to the altar to pray. I don't remember what I was praying about, but I know I was crying. Middle school is hard for everyone, and that is doubly true for little Black girls in predominantly non-Black schools who don't realize that racism isn't just something you see on the news. My body was overflowing with sadnesses I didn't have the language for, so I went to the altar and cried. When I was done, I shifted my weight to stand, but

someone came up from behind me and started to pray for me, so I stayed. Then I felt another set of hands. Then a few more. Before I knew it, I was surrounded. There might have been six people laying hands and praying for a breakthrough for me, and, honestly, all I was thinking about was if there would be any mac and cheese left by the time they were done. But I went with the flow. Hey, more Holy Ghost turn up for me, amiright? It all became very trancelike, lots of swaying and overlapping chants, and someone told me to speak.

They meant "to speak in tongues," but the last bit was unsaid. I had never done that before, but for years I had seen people doing it. My mom and all my friends' moms spoke in tongues during the Sunday worship services. It was a fruit of the spirit, and very much a rite of adolescent Pentecostal passage. A few of my friends had done it, and they got massive props. When a young person spoke in tongues, it felt like a badge of honor for the church community. Another young soul redeemed from depravity! Huzzah! And I guess someone believed that that Friday would be my day.

But what to say? What to do? How do you just speak the

language of immortals? Where could I find such an ancient sound in my body? As I was trying to figure out the logistics, some of the other people around me joined in, encouraging me to speak. They had no idea the gymnastics I was doing with my soft palate, and it was irrelevant. To them it was just me and God (and all six of them and a rogue church mom, who was now staring from the back of the sanctuary). I knew I couldn't disappoint them. These people had all missed out on mac and cheese for me. So I opened my mouth. And scatted.

Like a young Louis Armstrong, I skibiddy-bop shoo-bop-bop-skadap'ed my way into a thunderous applause. So I continued, this time with more confidence. *Skabop-skadap-sha-bibbity-bop*, and the tears started rolling, and the hallelujahs poured forth, and they all thanked God for the gift he had given me, and I thanked him, too, because clearly, I had arrived. We all hugged, I said my thank-yous to everyone for helping me get to my moment, and all the kids that remained ran downstairs with me to eat before all the food was either cold or gone.

When I look back on this story, I realize a couple of things:

- My Leo moon placement has always been front and center.
- Nobody in that sanctuary listened to jazz music, because I was basically a tone-deaf Ella Fitzgerald with no background singers.
- None of these people wanted my truth.

To them, I was a secondary character in my own spiritual breakthrough—but I had no control over that. There is a heavy performative aspect to Pentecostal Christianity, and I did what I needed to do to be accepted in that moment. I sacrificed my authentic self for a sense of community and praise.

Now that I think about it, I realize that the primary person who didn't want my truth was me. As a Black woman, you can be a lot of things, but weak is not one of them. If I had asked to leave the prayer huddle that day, I would've been called "scared" of the potential power of God. During those middle school years, I had no idea how much I had absorbed the expectations to embody "strong Black womanhood." Yes, I was allowed to cry, but only if I was overcome by the knee-crippling grace and love of white Jesus. I wanted to play, dance, sing, and be an idiot like all the other children, but I was never seen as a girl in the eyes of many of the congregants. I was a woman, and my Black womanhood needed parameters. My seventh-grade Missionettes teacher was an old white lady named Mrs. Hansen, who was also the first person to ever call me "disruptive," because I wanted to know if the Royal Rangers were taught how to wash their faces to prevent acne as extensively as we were. I was confused and angered by the accusation, for reasons I didn't quite understand, but I knew I had to keep my cool. A Black girl getting upset at an old white lady is never a good look. Strong emotions not centered around the Lord are allowed for others, but not for us. They are a sign of weakness, and we're not permitted that in these parts. Parameters.

My great-grandmother's name was Evelyn, and she lived in the mountains of Trelawny, Jamaica. My aunt, who was raised by her, told me that mama-Evelyn used to sing to her in a foreign tongue. It was a language that floated like the scent of freshly peeled mangoes in the midafternoon breeze— sweet, familiar, and welcoming.

It took generations for our family to realize that she was a Maroon, singing lullabies passed down from pre-slavery Ghana. Now, remembering that day in church, I think about mama-Evelyn. How no one knew what she was singing and that was okay: she knew. I tell myself that as I sat on the grimy carpet, surrounded by well-meaning congregants, with Hillsong playing on a loop in the background, she was with me, also encouraging me to speak. Not for them. But for us. So maybe I did. Maybe I skibibitty-bopped the words my soul needed to say that day. Maybe I did have a spiritual awakening, one they never could've planned or hoped for. Maybe, in the deepest part of me, mama-Evelyn and all my mothers before her were bursting with sweet water, dancing somewhere beautiful, proud that their newest daughter had finally freed her jaw and unleashed something wild into the world.

Honestly, I could be speaking all this out of my ass. Who knows? But, in retrospect, I did leave that sanctuary feeling more elated and accepted than when I'd entered. A lot of that was probably because I had given the prayer warriors what they had been hoping for, but, nevertheless, I felt accepted.

It was one of the few times I can remember being celebrated for being the odd one out. In that moment, running down the stairs to stuff my face with cold food, I didn't feel "strong" or "invincible" or "weak" or "fragile"—I just felt free, which might have been my homecoming after all.

Encouraging you to be chaotically yours,

SHAYNA CONDE
JERSEY CITY, NEW JERSEY

DEAR MCSWEENEY'S,
I want to tell you about my car. It's a 1998 Toyota Corolla that I've owned for ten years. In fact, our anniversary is next month. A decade together. I like that my car had a life before we met. I imagine the adventures it must have gone on before settling down with me. It was originally from West Virginia and had only eighty thousand miles on it when I bought it, despite being thirteen years old at that point.

How we found each other was, I knew a guy who restores and sells vintage Porsches. He's a "car guy." So I told him I wanted to buy a used car. Originally I thought maybe a Volvo. But he had a lead on this Corolla. I bought it off a woman for $2,500 in cash I'd strategically withdrawn from the bank before we met. It was probably worth more, with its low mileage, but I was there and I had cash so we made a deal.

What an investment. Though, to be honest, my car is falling apart. It's always burned oil pretty fast, so I have to keep pouring oil in. Both the back seat interior door handles have broken off. I need to get them replaced, though it's rare that I have a passenger back there. When I do, I have to open the door for them from the outside, like a chauffeur.

The Corolla appears frequently in my fiction. My forthcoming collection originally had mentions of Corollas in several stories, so I had to change some of them to other car models, like the Honda Civic, the Subaru Outback, the Ford Explorer. Just so people don't think it's the same Corolla in all the stories. Because then they might think the Corolla had some deeper meaning. Corollas as Easter eggs. Which wouldn't be such a bad thing, except that there is no deeper meaning. It's just the car I happen to own, and over the years it's become seared into my psyche, so it's the first car I think of, the image that springs to mind when I hear the word *car*.

It's important not to have names of things or people repeated in different stories in a collection. I had to make a list. I had some recurring Steves and Daves. My second Taco Bell reference was flagged, so I changed it to Hardee's. Then there are words with various possible spellings, and it's important to keep those consistent, I'm told. The copy editor made a style sheet for my book. Here is part of the list:

bandana, BART, Benelli (shotgun), BDSM, anti-gravity, Billabong (brand), Bikram yoga, CrossFit, dish towel, duffel bag, deer-like, DNR (Department of Natural Resources), Democratic Socialists of America, EpiPen, hipbone, hotspot, Johnnie Walker Black, Juul, Lululemon, *McSweeney's Quarterly Concern*, Muscle Milk, M&M's, Moleskine, meta-linguistics, Red Hot Chili Peppers (band), Paleo diet, trashcan, Sublime (band), popsicle, Sudoku, snapback (n), ribcage, SoulCycle, Shop-Vac, Tool (band), Stool (cover band), seatbelt, Styrofoam, Turing test, turnoff (n), Tapatío, X-rays, Zeppelin (Led), WWII

Anyway, for years everyone has made fun of me for having a car that's falling apart, with its unquenchable thirst for oil, its paint corroded from sea air,

its "power windows," which my passengers are forbidden to roll down, because they often won't roll back up. Once, an unknown person attacked the car with a crowbar or other implement and left some serious dents in the roof. Another time I found a cinder block under the right side of my car and noticed that all the lug nuts had been removed from one wheel. I had to walk over to the tire place, where a man gave me two lug nuts to put on so I could drive the car over to him. I walked back to the Corolla with the lug nuts in my pocket. It felt like a fairy tale.

Then recently we had that atmospheric river in San Francisco. I had parked my car on the street right beneath my window, since it was a Sunday and meters weren't enforced. All day, while I was in my living room writing or whatever, the rain was coming down hard. Then my boyfriend arrived and texted me from his truck: "The storm drain is clogged by your car and is forming a huge puddle and a tree branch fell next to it but your car is fine. We have to move your car." I looked out the window and my car was in a huge puddle with a big tree branch behind it. I mean the right side of the car, against the curb, was submerged in over a foot of water. So I moved it and since then the radio doesn't work and the floor is soaked and it smells like mildew. We tried putting baking soda all over the floor but it just formed a paste. I'm not sure what to do about all that.

I could get a newer car, but the thing is, I barely ever drive. I take the Corolla to Safeway once a week to buy groceries. I drive it to campus for the class I teach, but I could easily bike or take the bus. I like that my car is paid off, gets good gas mileage, and doesn't have any creepy technology. It's strictly analog, no-frills (aside from the power windows), which has made me a better driver. One time my dad was at a snooty cocktail party and other people were bragging about what their adult kids were doing these days, and when it was my dad's turn he said, "My daughter is *really* good at parallel parking." My parking skills have brought pride to my family. All thanks to the Corolla.

Now that there's some issue with semiconductor shortages due to the pandemic, used cars are in high demand. In fact, over the past six months, two strangers have offered to buy my car. One guy called out to me from the next car while we were stopped at a light. He said he was looking to buy a

car like mine for his niece. He said such cars were virtually impossible to find and buyers like himself would pay way over Blue Book value. He was very polite. I said okay, good to know. A few weeks later I found a note on my car with a similar offer and a person's phone number. It made me value my Corolla more, to know other people wanted it, and so, paradoxically, these offers made me less inclined to sell it. It made me feel very smug about the choices I had made. But that was before the atmospheric river and the seemingly ineradicable wetness inside my Corolla.

So for now I will hang on to my car and gradually decay alongside and within it. Sometimes, in the golden hour, I happen upon my Corolla standing in a picturesque setting, and imagine it in a magazine ad from 1998. In that way and others, we keep the spark alive.

Yours always,

KATE FOLK
SAN FRANCISCO, CA

DEAR MCSWEENEY'S,
I've experienced the joy and anguish that come with reentering the world of a novel after a few months' hiatus. After speaking to seasoned novelists

who confirmed that it never gets easier, I began to contemplate what it means to willingly pursue the artistic life, and so, as such thoughts tend to stifle my creative process, I'd taken a break to travel as a means of inspiration (or distraction?). These journeys led me to contemplate other matters too. Specifically, I've been pondering the invisible. What it means to see with the imaginative eye, to quiet our minds long enough to "see" beyond our present reality.

My husband and I had the opportunity to visit the Italian city of Turin this summer. We roamed the streets on the evening we arrived. The city felt either empty or crowded, depending on what stretch we walked. Not wanting to be perceived as rude foreigners, we smiled and greeted passersby, speaking the Italian greetings we knew. They averted their gazes. As we had lived in DC, big-city aloofness was not strange or unfamiliar to us; however, there seemed to be something nuanced in this lack of exchange. We felt a sense of despair cloaking the city, as unmistakable as it was elusive, and we kept asking ourselves, "What is that? What are we feeling?" We happened upon a park that looked like it had suffered a rough summer: Yellowing or dead grass; browning, scraggly bushes; split and contorted tree trunks with branches denuded of leaves. We heard little laughter, and the people, who had long and worn faces, did not appear to be enjoying their surroundings. They sat motionless on benches or were languorous in their movements. The park felt like a reflection of the city, which carried an austere joylessness. After returning to our hotel, we came across an article from the *New York Times* titled "The Ghosts of Turin," and we were stunned to discover evidence of what we might have dismissed or chalked up to jet lag. The article's author, Nikil Saval, writes:

> One of Turin's... notable features [is] its weird association with magic, madness and the occult. Here was where a troubling number of artists and philosophers had suffered crippling depressions or existential crises, or had gone crazy: the epic poet Torquato Tasso; the young Jean-Jacques Rousseau; the novelist Primo Levi. It was on or near the wide, trolley-crossed thoroughfare Via Po where Nietzsche famously saw a horse being maltreated, rushed to embrace it and then collapsed, suffering a fit of madness from which he would never recover.

We talked into the night about what one can truly "see" if one relinquishes the belief that what lies in front of us is all that exists. There is a multiplicity to the invisible, we decided. There is seeing in a new city that which lies beneath the surface of the sensible—what you can see, hear, smell, and touch. There is also seeing beyond your novel-in-progress's inchoate form to its completed version. It is a marvel how deep the invisible goes, like dipping your toe into a lake, uncertain of its depth. Who knows whether that inexplicable feeling we had as we walked through Turin was connected to the sufferings of other artists or to the historical trauma behind the scenes of a "crazy" city?

The invisible can overwhelm us, fill us with trepidation. But, if one allows it to, it can also encourage compassion. As I see an elderly waiter in Turin shuffling across the cobbled streets carrying plates of discarded pizza crusts and bits of linguine, I imagine an entire life story for him: his tiny flat overlooking a mercato, his ailing and beautifully aging wife, the estranged daughter with whom he has not spoken in years.

Khošāl Khān Khaṭak, Afghanistan's national poet, penned the lines "Know thou well this world its state, what is, is; what is not, is not." My rejoinder to Khaṭak's existential refrain is "What is, is not; and what is not, is." That which seems to us a certain way is frequently not, and often what we consider to be absent is actually present. My novel in its current state *is not* (though it is). But my novel in its completed form most certainly *is* (though it is not).

So travel has failed, ultimately, as a means of distraction. It has only returned me to what the late luminary Toni Morrison called the nonsecular and mysterious process of writing. Here I am again: at my desk, facing down a manuscript, envisioning both the world of the novel and a world in which the novel is complete.

In sight,

AFABWAJE KURIAN
IOWA CITY, IA

PELICAN PARADISE

by Nicky Gonzalez

THERE'S A TALL MAN in the frozen aisle. He is framed, from where I'm standing, by a tiled backdrop of boxed microwavable meals. His T-shirt reads I DON'T NEED GOOGLE. I HAVE MY WIFE, and stretches to translucence over the slope of his pregnant belly. Through the fabric, I can see the pucker of his belly button. An outie. I hope it's a beer gut or that he really is pregnant, that there is a hamster-sized human nestled in there, slowly growing. The alternative—that he's one of them: a doomed dad, a modern marvel—is too sad to consider. He holds a different brand of prepackaged cheeseburger in each hand, weighs his options.

I'm here for smoothing serum. The bottles on the shelf before me come in every shape and color. Words recur:

INSTANT! LIGHTWEIGHT! CAREFREE! If my father were here, I'd ask him how he dealt with these curls. His loose coils, which would have been gray by now, gleam light brown in pictures. My hair is that same shade—like cardboard, a friend once said—and looks stupid in the security mirror.

The man walks past me. I grab the cheapest bottle of goop and give it a whiff. It smells harsh enough to subdue my frizz, so I palm it and follow him to the checkout line. The man waggles his cheeseburger at his side. The plastic wrapper crinkles like static.

"Are you one of them guys?" the cashier asks. Her face is more freckled than not.

"My wife is due in a couple of weeks." Hot breath leaves my mouth, a gust from the sour and empty desert of my stomach. The man rubs his belly, though we all know that on the big day, like my father, he'll give birth to nothing. It's his family who'll do all the work once he's gone from the world.

He pushes a couple of bills toward the cashier, but she folds her arms and says, "No way. Burger's on me."

He thanks her and waddles over to the microwave to zap his food melty.

I pay for the hair stuff with the twenty Aunt June gave me and watch the man leave through the sliding-glass door. In the parking lot, he meets up with a woman wearing a bathing suit cover-up that's orange but fancy. She's going in on a key lime ice cream cone from Mrs. G's, shaping her tongue into a small shovel and lapping up chunks. This must be her, the wife who's smarter than Google. They face each other and talk through mouthfuls. Their swollen bellies, twin curves, are almost touching.

The wife catches me staring and waves. I shift my eyes to the palm tree behind her and pretend I've been watching a crane the whole time. Hand in hand, they head toward Pelican Paradise. They must be tourists, renting one of the nice trailers down on Avocado Lane. I want to go back to June's, but I don't want to seem like I'm following them. I skim through a magazine to kill time. Nessie has been spotted once more. Someplace where people climb mountains and eat sausage for every meal, a man found a cursed ring on the ground. A kid in Kentucky caught a ghost on camera. The magazine cover assures me that I can count on it, week to week, to report on the world's wonders.

At Pelican Paradise Mobile Home Park, June's double-wide squats a hundred feet behind the high tide mark. Its faded blue planks almost always match the sky. June is sitting in the entryway, spritzing a spot of carpet. A blotch of sweat the size of my hand stains the back of her halter top. Her paper towel goes down white, comes up slightly yellowed.

"Bongo peed," she says.

I step over her. Bongo is in the living room and he twirls onto his back when he sees me. His head hangs off the couch in a way that can't be comfortable. There's no remorse on his upside-down face.

When June is done cleaning, she takes Bongo for a run on the beach. I tell her I'm too busy to join. She holds up Bongo's leash and he wriggles in his spot like a liquid before shooting toward her. With a two-pound weight in each hand and the leash handle draped around her wrist, June power walks out the door. June is sixty-something and has more energy than I do. My dad, her nephew, was like a son to her. Sometimes, when she stares at me for too long, I can tell she sees him somewhere in my face. I don't like it.

Once June is gone, I rush into my summer bedroom. The fluorescent tube light above the dresser mirror is hospital harsh; every distended pore gets screen time. This was once my father's room, and aside from a few dresser drawers that June has cleared out for me, it's a slice of his childhood frozen in time. Summers with June are like archaeological digs, visits to the Museum of Dad. In an old popcorn tin, there are hardened tubes of sunscreen and rash creams that are older than I am. I study their packaging regularly. Maybe my father coated his neck with SPF 50 and caught whiffs of artificial coconut throughout the day. Maybe he had eczema. I found Mom's journals last year, in a box tucked into the corner of her bedroom. According to her entries, his favorite drink was Yoo-hoo, and his aftershave left his cheeks waxy to the touch. The details I've plucked from his room, from the journals, piece together to create a mosaic of a man.

I work three squirts of hair slime into my puffy ends. After ten minutes of smoothing and scrunching, my hair looks less luminous than it does greasy. A familiar voice floats in through an open window. Resting my arms on the windowsill, I peek out at a world so sun-drenched that at first, I see only bright white shapes. The pregnant couple from earlier walk with folded towels squished under their curled arms, beach bags whacking their hips with each step.

"I told you to hang it up after you used it yesterday," the man says, lowering his nose to the towel he's holding. "Now it smells."

"Who cares? We can trade."

Maybe the beach isn't such a bad idea. I pull on a one-piece that's covered in palm leaves. Looking in the mirror, I run my hands down my sides in hopes that I'll discern some dip at the center, some hint at a waist. Pubes stick out from the suit's crotch. The black tufts are like beacons. If someone looked at me now, they'd see only pubes. A pair of basketball shorts do the trick. Plus, the baggy pants legs magic my hips a bit wider. The screen door whooshes shut behind me.

At the beach, I slide my sandals off and scan the dunes. Behind a cluster of saw grass, the couple flatten their towels side by side. June jogs along the tide line as Bongo, enraged, bites at sea foam. I jog to meet her, and together we pull seaweed from Bongo's mouth. Farther along the beach, a seagull dive-bombs an old woman's meal and ascends with a slice of white bread in its beak.

"So you decided to come out," June says brightly.

When I started middle school, Mom and Aunt June began

applauding me whenever I got out of bed, brushed my teeth, washed a spoon. I've spent every summer since I was six in Islamorada, but Mom was shocked when, one morning last month, I asked when she'd be dropping me off at June's. I was squished next to her in the bathroom mirror, trying to iron my hair while she brushed her teeth. The smell of burned plastic—a sign that my curls were flattening according to plan under the iron's heat—had us breathing through our mouths. "Honey," Mom shouted. "I'm so glad you still want to go. I thought maybe you were too—I don't know. Too old for that now." My guess is that once I turned thirteen, Mom and June both assumed I'd stop showing signs of life.

June smiles now the same way Mom did that morning, warm surprise in her eyes. The surf swallows then spits out our feet as we pad along the sand. Bongo pees on a crab. "Look at that," I say. When there is more focus on me than I would like, nothing deflects attention better than a dog.

"You know, your dad picked this sweet little monster out from the shelter," June says, nudging Bongo.

I do know. June tells me the story every summer and she tells it again now. Every time my family brings up my father—the time he mistook bacon fat for eggnog, the domino table he'd pull from the closet and carry with him to parties—I listen. Every version of every story is filed away.

June tells Bongo's adoption story with the same flare in the same parts, with the same jokes and asides as always. According to June, my parents packed up for the Keys the moment they discerned their matching bumps. She says Carlos couldn't let his aunt Juney go on not knowing.

My dad worried that June wouldn't leave her bed for months after he died, the way she had when his mother passed. He thought a fuzzy companion might help. He drove June to an animal shelter in Key Largo, and when they saw Bongo, only a year old, with giant paws he had yet to grow into and his wide pit bull smile, they fell instantly in love.

"The night we brought Bongo home, your mom dropped a whole chicken breast on the floor and he slurped it up. I mean, it was gone in two seconds," June finishes. She howls at her own story with her signature laugh.

In the journals I've snooped through, my mother writes about standing in front of my father, looking down at their sloped bellies, her heart dropping. I imagine that my parents hooked hands and cried. I imagine my father panicking, wishing I wasn't doing this to him. When my father rubbed his palm over his belly and swore he felt a slight bump, he must have prayed for it to not be true. As my fingernails grew and my bones swelled in their sockets, my father braced himself for my mother's due date. When he determined roughly on which day he would die, he must have clung tight to the ones he loved and eaten arepas for every meal. Whited-out passages dot the remainder of that journal. Whole swaths, sometimes entire pages, are pale as eggshells. When I hold them up to the light, there's only the faintest hint of the ink below.

My own journals are always stop-and-start. I fill them

for two straight weeks and then abandon them for a year. Sometimes I read them back and am surprised by what past-me has written: a two-day crush on Christian Ortega, over the course of which I "smelled his body odor, which kind of turned me on"; Mom correcting me while I filled out a family tree assignment (June was my great-aunt, not my aunt-aunt). What can people forget in a decade? What made Mom, years after filling those pages, act as her own censor?

Bongo bounds toward the pregnant couple and leaps in circles around them. The woman has just cracked open a plastic takeout container and Bongo licks his lips, whimpering.

June jogs over to them, shouting "Sorry" every other step. I trudge after her. My thighs burn from speed-walking on the beach. June kneels and hugs Bongo to her chest. Her eyes fall on the man's belly, and for a second she looks so sad I want to plunge my head into the hot sand.

"You guys from around here?" June asks. It's a leading question. No one ever is.

"Miami," the woman says.

"Coral Gables," the man specifies. "You?"

June gestures at the trailers. "Right over there. I've been in Islamorada my whole life. This is my niece, Yami. She's visiting from Miami too."

I want the couple to think I might be fancy, so I don't correct her by saying I'm from Hialeah. They tell June they're staying nearby in a double-wide on Avocado Lane.

"One of those B and Bs on the internet?" June asks.

The man nods.

"It's called an Airbnb, Juney," I mutter.

The woman forks a limp sliver of fish into her mouth. Bongo thrashes in June's arms. His tail wags on its highest setting. June talks to the couple in that open way she has. If you give her ten minutes with any stranger, she'll become their best friend. We learn that the woman's name is Jeannine and the man's name is Oscar. I seesaw on my heels and toes, sinking as far as I can into the sand without lifting my feet. Oscar's stomach is covered with swirls of dried sunscreen.

"You know, Yami's dad was a pregnant father just like you," June says.

"What are the odds?" Jeannine says.

"Low, but not impossible," I say. The research is still young, but from the forums I lurk in, I know there are more than a few of us who've been touched by this rare phenomenon. There's Xenomorph4Evr, who doesn't post so much now that their partner, Andy, has died, and RedTabby89, who found out her boyfriend was cheating after he could no longer hide his belly with baggy shirts. Others post their theories—it's the pH of the water, microwave radiation—but they're just guessing. For all my hours of research, I'm certain of awfully little.

Jeannine smiles at me. She has so many teeth. "Your dad would be so proud to see you now. So, so beautiful."

There's nothing pretty about me. I'm hairy in the wrong places and I have yet to grow a butt. I blush.

June invites them over for a taco dinner, but they have reservations at Pierre's. We're welcome at their rental anytime, they say. It's the mint-colored house with orange trim. Impossible to miss. June shakes their hands and I wave from where I stand, ankle deep in sand, avoiding Oscar's eyes.

If he chooses to get an ultrasound, the technician will point to the empty, bean-shaped darkness of his would-be womb. The body his family will bury will be flat-bellied, as though he'd really given birth to something, and his kid will forever nurse the feeling that they've done something wrong.

That night, June and I watch *Jeopardy!* while we have dinner on the couch. June sweeps the European geography category. I answer one question. Oil and onions drop from my tortilla. The dishes at Pierre's are probably artfully plated with thin steak slices and smears of chimichurri, portions that would leave anyone wanting.

I leave June's in the morning, my face freshly scrubbed, and head toward Avocado Lane. The couple was right. Their rental is unmistakable, mint with orange garnishes. It looks more like a cake than a house. I ring their doorbell and knock a few times.

Jeannine throws the door open. She's wearing a fluffy green robe. Her hair is pulled back in a tight bun. She's filled in her eyebrows, but the rest of her face is untouched. I make a mental note to buy a brow pencil. "Oh," she says. "Yami, right?"

I nod.

"Do you need something?"

"You said I could drop by."

Over her shoulder, there's a clock on the wall that looks like the inside of an aquarium. The minute hand cuts in front of a clown fish. It's 7:38. Suddenly, I want more than anything to fold into myself like a hermit crab. Maybe I should turn and run back to June's. If I bump into Jeannine again, I'll duck behind a car or camouflage myself in front of a mural.

"Come in," she says. "We're gonna check out Rain Barrel in a bit, if you wanna come."

She leads me into the kitchen and asks me to sit while she and Oscar get ready in the next room. If I want, she says, I can take a soda from the fridge. I check out the selection. They only have weird flavors: rhubarb, elderflower, hibiscus. I don't know if I'd like those, so I reach into the back and grab one called Berry Blast. It's tart and sweet. On the counter, there's a loaf of bread that looks like it's made solely of seeds. Their peanut butter has a thick layer of oil on top, and I wonder if it's gone bad as I chug my bright red drink.

Jeannine enters the kitchen, casual and glamorous in a loose shirt that looks softer than any of my blankets. Oscar sits by me at the table. "I hear you'll be joining us today," he says. "It'll be nice to have a tour guide."

"I've been coming here since I was a baby," I hear myself say.

Oscar wrinkles his nose and looks at my soda. "Where did you get that?"

"The fridge."

"Shit," Jeannine says. She grabs the bottle and reads it. "Five percent. Other renters must've left it." She upends the bottle over the sink, and the remains glug down the drain.

"You'll be fine," Oscar says, handing me a water.

I've never been drunk before, so I'm not sure if I am now. When I rest my face, my mouth settles into a slight smile. Jeannine and Oscar decide I need something in my stomach, so to Bob's Bunz we go, where I order a cinnamon roll the size of my head. By the time we get to the shops at Rain Barrel, I'm licking icing off the crumpled wax paper. Jeannine hands me her phone and asks me to take a picture of her and Oscar under a sculpture of a giant lobster. Its monstrous head towers above their faces as they pose: they give the camera a thumbs-up; they point at antennae the length of hockey sticks; they hug, twin bellies touching. Seeing something that should be no bigger than my forearm blown up to a thousand times its size makes my stomach twist. Magnified like this, the lobster looks like an extraterrestrial cockroach, something you'd have to squash on a spaceship.

Oscar swipes through the photos as Jeannine leads us through the shops. I've never been to Rain Barrel. It's an "artisan village," which means tourists can come buy knick-knacks adorned with all kinds of fish. The shops are nestled between trees, and it's nice to be in the shade. In an art gallery, we squint at glass sculptures—a ballerina en pointe, gorgonian coral, countless crystal butterflies. I lean in close to a sculpture that's an abstract swirl. *Bird of Paradise*, the label says. I don't get it.

Oscar comes over with a stiff paper shopping bag in his hand. He asks me what my favorite piece is, and I point at *Bird of Paradise* to seem sophisticated. "Interesting," he says. He nods down at the bag. "We got the coral." Jeannine is next door, looking at handmade journals. Standing under hanging macramé slings that cradle globes of sea glass, Oscar asks me what grade I'm in and where I go to school. I answer his questions: rising eighth grader, Filer Middle.

"You're a Panther," he says. "Me too."

"I thought you lived in Coral Gables."

"Grew up Hialeah, though. Right by the Walgreens on Mango Hill. Is Mr. LaGuerre still teaching algebra?"

I shake my head and think of someone we could connect over. "Dr. Ferguson is pretty old," I say. Oscar remembers him. We exchange impressions of Dr. Ferguson's raspy, angry voice while turning conch shells in our hands. On the walk home, Oscar and Jeannine ask about my best subjects, my favorite books. All day, everyone they pass has glanced first at Oscar's belly, then at Jeannine's. Some give a flat, awkward smirk, as though to say, *This is the smile I'd give any stranger*. Most look away and pretend they haven't just seen a dead man walking.

It's almost one o'clock when I get back to June's. As I glop imitation-crab dip onto some crackers for lunch, June asks me where I've been all day. "You were gone before I even woke up. I was gonna make you eggs in a hole," she says.

I tell her I've been hanging out with the pregnant couple.

"They seem so nice, those two," she says. "Hey, wanna go to Theater of the Sea one of these days?"

"Could we invite Oscar and Jeannine?" I ask.

"I don't know about that. They don't have much time left together. We shouldn't pressure them to see a bunch of sea lions dancing if they don't want to."

"We can just ask. They don't have to say yes. We can ask them tonight."

"Do you three have dinner plans?"

"No, but they said we could stop by whenever."

June's face falls into the shape it does when she sees my father in me. She tucks a curl behind my ear and smooths my eyebrow with her cold thumb. I rub the sensation away with the heel of my hand. After some negotiation, June agrees that it'd be okay to invite the couple to go snorkeling at the state park.

Before the snorkeling tour, we kill time by browsing the exhibits in the visitor center. Backlit fish tanks built into the wall glow in the dim room. There are funky shrimp, tiny jellyfish. TVs line the back wall. On one screen, there's a time-lapse video of coral blooming into florets on a rock. On another, a seahorse curls its tail around the tendril of a sea whip to anchor itself in place. It heaves and heaves. On each exhale, dozens of specks fly from his belly like snot particles in a sneeze. The babies make my skin crawl. They pour forth and wriggle like maggots in the water. I lose count of how many times I watch the video loop.

I sunscreen my shoulders by the swamp-side pavilion. Oscar and Jeannine are nearby, rubbing the waxy leaves of a sea grape tree between their fingers. Oscar rips one off and uses it to fan Jeannine's face. A dozen kids my age trot past me toward the dock. They all speak at once, through mouthfuls of greasy breakfast sandwiches and powdered doughnuts. Some kind of summer camp, I guess. I hum a bit to prep my vocal cords in case one of them talks to me.

When we get on the boat, I put on my flippers and life vest. The vest makes my top half even boxier and, with the flippers on, I walk with high knees like a crane. Oscar sits next to me and secures his clasp so the strap rests loosely on his stomach.

Our tour guide, Aaron, introduces himself to us as we cruise along the calm water. The tableau that scrolls by seems like the same twenty feet of forest repeating itself endlessly: the mangroves' tangled roots like countless limbs frozen mid-handshake. Aaron names and describes families of coral, rattling off descriptions of alien beauty in the rote way a server might recite the daily specials.

"Look," Oscar says, leaning close and pointing at an osprey. "Pretty doofy, huh?"

"Yeah," I say. "That bird has no idea what's going on."

When the boat exits the winding channels of the mangrove forest and heads into the open sea, we accelerate. We bounce in our seats until we're three miles out and the boat is anchored. Aaron gives a short speech on ocean safety for snorkeling beginners.

I shield my eyes with a flat hand and look into the water. Bright reds and oranges wobble under the ocean's surface. We have an hour. Aaron tells us that to see fish and other critters, we should stay still for ten minutes. Once our splashes have settled, angelfish will wiggle their pancake bodies out of crevices; hermit crabs will sprout from their shells and ticker away.

Everyone lets Oscar and Jeannine get out first. They make their painstaking way down the ladder. June and I jump in after them, and the two of us flipper toward a big coral cluster. When we get to it, we take Aaron's advice and float in place. A sea worm inches out from under brain coral. Fluorescent fans jut from its back like a ruffled sleeve. It's both beautiful and gross.

I lift my head and ask June if there's a bathroom on the boat.

"What?"

I pop the snorkel out of my mouth and repeat the question.

"Do you have to pee?" she asks.

I nod.

"Me too. Let's just do it."

June counts down from three and we release our own warmth into the Atlantic. When we're done, June grabs my arm and pulls me away from the scene of the crime in search of new creatures. Jeannine and Oscar float nearby, flipper to flipper like lovebugs, baring only the backs of their orange vests to the sun.

When I plunge my face under the water, I can see their arms at rest, curving down toward the reef. An arm's distance from them, a barracuda sneers at Oscar. My legs propel me forward, and soon I'm waving my arm under Jeannine's face. We pop our heads out of the water—one, two, three—faces squinched by goggles, cheeks puffed around mouthpieces. I pull them away and tell them what I saw. When we're at a safe distance, the three of us submerge ourselves again and gaze in the direction from which we swam. There it is, with its tremendous underbite and its torpedo body. For what remains of the tour, I patrol the waters, certain now that the reefs beneath us are teeming with primordial carnivores.

On the ride back, we sway in the slow-moving boat, each sitting in our own puddles of saltwater drip. Aaron tells us it's a myth that barracudas often attack humans. They follow snorkelers and divers around, he says, because they think we're large predators and hope to scavenge the remains of our prey. I picture Oscar floating facedown, his eyes closed, no bubbles creeping from the corners of his lips, a pack of barracudas feasting on the man we've left behind.

After the tour, when we're back on the pebbly asphalt of the parking lot, I ask what we're having for dinner. "I'm thinking enchiladas or lasagna," I say. Something big we can bake, so everyone can have their fill. Jeannine picks at her ear and glances over her shoulder at the mangroves and their roots that spread like petticoat wires.

"I can make you and me some enchiladas if that's what you want, sweetie," June says.

When we get to the parking lot, Oscar and Jeannine wish us goodnight. We leave in separate cars.

The week passes slowly. Time is gelatinous here; a planned hour of reading stretches into three or five. People sip Lime-a-Ritas on the beach as hot gusts roll in from the ocean and lull them to sleep. I knock on Jeannine and Oscar's door every day. Sometimes they aren't home. Sometimes they let me in and we share key lime cookies from a greasy Bob's Bunz bag. Sometimes I stroll with them along the shore without saying much, because I'm happy just to be nearby. I start writing in my journal again. One night, sitting on the beach, I fill pages with the things I've done that day: had a hot dog for breakfast, told the boy at the stand I didn't have a cell phone when he asked for my number, joined Jeannine and Oscar at the diving museum and took pictures of them wearing old-timey scuba masks. It's eight-ish and the sky is purple. My shorts are still damp from swimming with June earlier. I lie back on my towel and fold my hands over my stomach. If Oscar were here, he'd make this moment fun. We'd joke while hurling seashells like Frisbees at the nearest palm. My chest and arms grow warm, and I smile up at the handful of stars that puncture the sky. But there's a baby on the way. The quick curdling of my good mood shocks me.

After I found Mom's journals last year, I'd sit with a sleeve of crackers and read them from the moment I got home from school to the moment I heard her car growling in the drive-way. I held the whited-out pages up to the lamplight and looked at the backs of them, but it was impossible to read what she'd blocked out. Now I think I can imagine what she wrote.

I close my eyes and run my hands through my salt-stiff hair. When I open them again, the stars have doubled. It feels like an ambush. I shake the sand out of my towel and head home.

June is making sloppy joes for lunch. I help her chop cabbage into strips for her famous crunchy slaw. Sitting cross-legged on the floor, we eat off the coffee table. Bongo licks at my calves like he's trying to get at something in the center. June wants to go to Theater of the Sea. She says one of these days she's gonna really treat us and get us passes to swim with the sea lions.

"Do you think Jeannine and Oscar want some sloppy joes?" I ask.

"Sure," June says. "Take a plate over to them."

I load a paper plate with two sandwiches and a moun-tain of slaw while June clears our dishes. My sneakers squeak all the way down to Avocado Lane, the ground still damp from a recent sun shower. The sight of the orange-and-mint house gets me speed-walking. Every second matters when you know your friend will soon disappear. I knock, wait, and knock again, try the door. It's open. The fish clock hums as the cadence of an argument floats from the bedroom.

"I just think that if we ask her nicely—"

"Have a heart, Oscar."

"I'm not answering the fucking door. Not today."

"Have you seen the way she looks at you?"

"It's too much, Jean. How much more time do you and I have left together?"

I can't hear Jeannine's answer.

"A week? A week and a half?"

"Oscar…"

"I'm just saying. This is supposed to be a vacation."

I leave the sloppy joes on their kitchen table next to the oily peanut butter and a new loaf of nasty seeded bread. There are three Berry Blasts left in the refrigerator. I tuck all of them into my waistband and slam the door on my way out. The bottles clink with every stomp, a wind chime in a storm. I press them to my belly and focus on the shock of cold glass against my skin until, under the cover of a banyan tree by US 1, I sit in the dirt.

The bottle tops are twist-off. Bubbles prickle the back of my tongue. An iguana side-eyes me from a branch as I chug. I waggle a fist at him, but he doesn't budge. The second bottle doesn't go down any smoother. When it's empty, I hurl it at the tree's trunk. It bounces off the bark unceremoniously, but when I throw the other one, it shatters. The iguana leaps to the ground and scurries across the road. The world seems to move faster, as though life were happening at a slower frame rate. I stand up and go to lean against one of the banyan's prop roots, but I miss, instead slamming hard against the ground. As though a button had been pressed, Berry Blast and sloppy joe stream from my mouth onto my shirt.

And then I'm off, jogging across US 1 to the gift shop. Tourists shield their noses as I pass them on my way to the clearance rack. They can all get fucked. "Suck my toes!" I shout to no one in particular. As I flip through each item on the rack in search of the steepest markdown, I make sure to drop all the baby clothes on the ground. The dressing room mirror is too clean. I'm hideous. No human being has ever looked this splotchy. I wrangle my hair into a ponytail and pull on the cheapest shirt I can find. It hangs past my knees and says BIKINI INSPECTOR across the chest. No matter. A shirt like this is standard out here. By wearing it, I'll become invisible. I wear it to the checkout counter, where the cashier scans the tag that hangs from the collar. On my way home, I stuff the dirty shirt deep into a roadside trash can.

I'm almost at June's when I see Oscar jogging toward me down a side street, holding a paper gift bag.

"Bikini inspector?" he says when he reaches me.

"Suck. My. Toes."

He steps toward me and holds out the bag. He says he doesn't know how much I heard, but he didn't mean most of what he said. He says I have to understand how stressed he is, how scared. And look, he says, he and Jeannine went out just yesterday to buy me a gift. I lift something heavy out of the bag and peel off the gift tissue. The swirls of glass from the art gallery, *Bird of Paradise*. I hate it more now than when I first saw it. The motion is second nature now. It's the same arc and force I used on the second bottle. The sculpture breaks into three chunks on the asphalt.

"I said fuck off," I say over my shoulder.

June is giving Bongo belly rubs and watching *Jeopardy!* reruns when I get home. She starts to ask what took me so long but stops when she sees me.

"Did you change clothes?" She walks over to me and presses her cold fingers to my forehead. "Sweetie, you look kind of sick."

It's the magnetic pull of her clammy hands to my skin, the way she can't help but love me, that finally makes my shoulders droop. I weep into June's neck. I tell her what happened as she squeezes me. She guides me to the couch and sits on the floor by my head. Alex Trebek asks a question about the 2014 Olympics. "Not now, Alex," June says. She turns the TV off and grabs my hand in both of hers. My eyes burn. Sleep pulls me closed.

It takes a few days for the fizz of my rage to settle. I will do the adult thing, I decide. I'll apologize. Cars zip past me on

US 1 as I jaywalk to the gift shop. Under a sign that says NEAT STUFF!, I find my olive branch: a tiny onesie I saw three days ago. The tag says 3–6 MONTHS, but Jeannine can put it aside until it fits. A marlin swims beneath the phrase SOMEONE IN ISLAMORADA LOVES ME! It's stupid, but I can't show up at Oscar and Jeannine's empty-handed.

On the walk to their trailer, I go over the things I want to apologize for. By the time I'm at their rental, I haven't listed half. The door is open a crack and a vacuum roars inside. I knock and yell hello. The vacuum hushes. A woman I don't recognize opens the door.

"Hey, sweetheart. What can I do for you?" she says.

"Are Oscar and Jeannine here?"

"The pregnant couple? They checked out this morning."

"Did they leave anything for a Yami?" I ask, twisting the shopping bag handles into a rope. "Did you find a note or something?"

She doesn't think so.

I cram the onesie into my pocket, go back to June's, and take Bongo for a walk on the beach. He circles me like a frenzied moon on the packed wet sand and I think that today, if he wants to crush a crab between his jaws, I'll let him. I give him one end of the onesie and he tugs. We play like this for a while, both of us fighting for something we don't even want. Any day now, Oscar will shiver and leave the world. As Jeannine gives birth, she'll squeeze his hand. She'll say goodbye and hello.

WHEN A MAN DIES
by ANNA AKHMATOVA

Translated by Katie Farris and Ilya Kaminsky

When a man dies,
his portraits change.
Different eyes stare at us, lips
stir in a stranger's smile.
I notice this, returning
from the funeral of a poet.
I often check it:
my theory's confirmed.

(1940)

DOG LAB

by T. C. BOYLE

For Joe Purpura

THE FLIGHT HE WAS on ran into heavy turbulence when the pilot started their descent, the kind of turbulence that brought up images of sheared metal, flaming jet fuel, and scattered body parts. Everybody aboard instantaneously went from the vague unease of airplane mode to full-on panic. The girl sitting next to him—a young mother he'd been flirting with ever since he put his anatomy text away—snatched her baby to her chest and molded her body into a shield. The plane dipped violently and shuddered through the length of it. Something thumped to the floor and rolled under his seat, the sound of it lost in the scream of the engines. He felt his heart rate spike and found himself fiercely gripping the arms of his seat as if he alone could steady the plane and bring them all home safely. "We're encountering a little rough patch here, folks," the pilot crooned redundantly from the cockpit. "Make sure your seat belts are securely fastened."

Afterward, when the plane was on the ground and the rain was lashing down as if they were parked under Iguazú Falls, the girl turned a ghostly face to him. "God, that was... I mean, I thought...," she managed before the baby supplied the rest with a single lung-rattling shriek. He said, "Yeah, me too." He was still trying to recover his equilibrium, never happier to be alive than in that moment. The pilot's voice came to them again and it was a voice he could have listened to forever, the voice of salvation, but what it had to say was utterly pedestrian, not to mention anticlimactic—there was an aircraft ahead of them at the gate and there would be a brief delay. In the next moment, the engines shut down on a vast collective silence riven only by the hiss of the rain. No one said a word. They were all still in shock.

That was when they heard the barking. From below them, in the hold, came the harsh, insistent complaint of a dog that had been caught in the same maelstrom they had. With the difference, of course, that the dog couldn't conceive of what had just happened or where it was or why. The dog had known only the lump of ground meat containing the sedative, then the last touch of its owner's hand, then the cage, then the drowsiness. And now it was awake to something else altogether, strange smells, darkness, the mechanical groans and whimpers of the plane settling around it.

Jackson was feeling disoriented himself—they all were—but they'd boarded the plane voluntarily and their cage was the aluminum shell sculpted overhead, familiar to them, expected, confinement a part of the price you had to pay to get where you were going. Not that it would have mattered to the dog—it was frightened, it was uncomfortable, it was caged. It barked and kept on barking. He pictured a big animal, deep-chested, a German shepherd or rottweiler or some such, its head thrown back, jaws snapping open and shut with each furious breath. Its distress preyed on him, especially after what he'd just gone through, what they'd all gone through. And why couldn't the pilot or the flight attendant or whoever take the initiative and switch on some music, anything, even the inane pop drivel they usually inflicted on their passengers?

The pilot came back on the intercom to inform them that he'd gotten word it would be another twenty minutes and to admonish them to remain seated with their seat belts fastened. His voice overrode the dog's and momentarily distracted them all from the animal's discomfort, which was different from theirs only in degree. But as soon as the intercom switched off, the dog's barking was right there again, front and center, working like a drill at their nerves.

"Poor dog," the girl said.

Beyond the rain-smeared window, somewhere inside the long, low terminal building that appeared as a dim glow against the night, was Juliana, who'd come to pick him up with the prospect of dinner and bed in their immediate future. She knew nothing of the near-death experience he'd just been through or of the young mother with her milk-swollen breasts and birdlike shoulders transforming herself into impregnable steel or of the desolate dog that just couldn't stop barking. "Yeah," he said, lighting and extinguishing a quick smile. "Poor us too."

One minute you're alive, the next you're dead—those were the conditions of the world, and even to attempt to assign any logic to them was to fall into the deep, dark vat of religion and other associated forms of voodoo. The plane could have crashed, transmuting himself, the young mother, her baby, and the bewildered dog into so many scraps of scorched meat, but it hadn't, and once he'd hugged Juliana to him and told her the story—it took all of thirty seconds—he forgot about it. Life was expendable, wasn't it? And it hadn't expended him yet, so what was the problem?

He thought he'd put it behind him, but when he went up the steps to the teaching hospital three days later, the barking of the dogs in the basement brought the scene back to him. The sound, faint and tympanic, was heavily muffled by the storm windows and the ancient stone walls, and it was so familiar it had long since become a kind of background noise to his daily progress up and down those steps, no different from the rasp of tires out on the boulevard or the chatter of the birds in the trees or the screech of brakes, but now it separated itself, and he pictured the dogs down there in their cages, awaiting their turns in Dog Lab, as uneasy and impatient as the dog in the cargo hold, except that dog had been going home and these weren't. He was in his third year of med school and his rotation had taken him through ob-gyn, pediatrics, and internal medicine, and surgery was next up on his schedule, which meant he'd be in intimate contact with those dogs soon enough. When he'd first mentioned this to Juliana a month ago, she'd made a face and said, "What you mean, *Dog Lab*? You're not going to be a veterinarian, are you, Jax?"

They were at her apartment on a study date, she at her desk in the corner, he on the couch, hunched over one of the twenty-pound texts he had to lug around with him everywhere he went, lest he should miss out on a precious undirected moment in which he could be studying. They'd been dating for the better part of the past year. Her apartment was a model of order and tasteful arrangement, like a stage set before the actors drift in from the wings; his was not. She cooked for him sometimes, and sometimes he spent the night, and they'd talked of moving in together and consolidating expenses, but because of their madhouse schedules (she was student teaching and working afternoons at Burger King, and for his part he couldn't tell the difference between med school and boot camp, except that boot camp was a whole lot shorter), they hadn't gotten around to it.

"No," he said, "I told you—it's part of the surgery rotation?"

She had her own massive text spread open before her, the gloss of its thick coated paper redirecting the light of her desk lamp every time she turned a page. "What do you mean?" she asked, glancing up at him. He could see from the way her eyes clicked like counters—one beat, two beats, three—that she was doing the math. "You're not going to... I mean, you don't *practice* on them, do you?"

If he'd had his own qualms, he was well past them now. He'd had a dog when he was a kid, and a cat, too, and he'd never intentionally inflicted pain on any creature, not even the cockroaches that erupted from the drain every time he turned the shower on and that met their fate quickly and decisively, but he nonetheless did what was required of him—and this was what was required. "How else are we going to learn physiology—I mean, outside of cadavers and a textbook? It's not like we can just take the elevator up to the OR and start doing heart surgery on somebody..."

She was silent. Behind her, on the flickering screen of the TV that she kept going through every waking hour as if it were her own personal life-support system, the massive lumpen head and vacant eyes of Gerald Ford advanced and receded as he took questions at a press conference, his mouth moving in dumb show because the sound was muted. He thought she was going to say something more, something along the lines of *Doesn't that bother you?*, but she didn't. She took up her turquoise marker and highlighted a passage in her text that was already highlighted in yellow. From the apartment above came the repetitive thump of the bass line to a tune he used to play with the R&B band he was in back when he had the time to devote to anything other than *Basic Neuroanatomy* or *Harrison's Principles of Internal Medicine*, and that pulled him out of himself long enough for her to drop the next question into the vacuum. "What happens to them when, you know, they've been, what, operated on?"

What happened was that they were euthanized and their blood was drained for use in veterinary clinics. He said, "I don't know."

"They kill them, don't they?"

Professor Ciotti had addressed the issue in Medical Ethics by pointing out that there were too many irresponsible dog owners in the world and too many unwanted dogs—the shelters couldn't begin to keep pace with the numbers they were presented with daily. If a dog wasn't adopted in two weeks, it was euthanized. Why not, Professor Ciotti asked, use them to benefit humanity?

He gave her a weak smile. He didn't like it any better than she did. "Yeah," he said, "I hate to say it, but they're going to put them down in the shelter anyway."

"So they're expendable, is that what you're saying?"

Behind her, President Ford had been replaced by a Ford Mustang, a convertible, red with black upholstery, a car he'd love to get his hands on someday. He watched it eat up S-turns on a deserted blacktop road, then sighed and slapped the book shut. "You know what?" he said. "I don't want to talk about it. I really don't."

The dog he was assigned—or, rather, that his group of three was assigned—was a beagle. It didn't have a name, or not that he knew of, anyway. There was no point in names. The dogs had been selected at the pound by one of the lab techs, an acromegalic giant by the name of Reggie, whom everyone called Lurch behind his back, after the character on the TV show, and if at some point the dogs had lived with families and wore collars and tags with their names engraved on them, no one knew about that either. They'd been abandoned. They were lab animals now and that was all anybody needed to know. "Don't think of them in terms of your family pets," Dr. Markowitz, the resident overseeing the surgery rotation, told them the first day. "Think of them in terms of a problem to be solved." He'd let out a low chuckle. "Which, if any of you do go on to become surgeons, is more or less how you'll have to think of your patients. Emotions have to be compartmentalized, and you shouldn't have to think about your first incision any more than your last. Practice makes perfect, and that is what this lab is all about."

There were three dogs laid out on separate operating tables, each attended by three students who would take turns rotating between prepping, assisting, and operating. His group consisted of Jerry Katz, whom he liked and respected and had even played pinball with once or twice at Herlihy's, a dive bar that was equally divided between med students and neighborhood types, and Paul Sipper, who'd gone to Yale and never let anybody forget it and was about as likable as a sealed jar on a high shelf.

The dogs had been prepped by Lurch and the other tech, an equally inimical figure who'd worked at the hospital for the past decade or maybe even longer, nobody knew, not even the nurses, and the nurses knew everything. His eyes were like drill presses—he'd seen every sort of fuckup imaginable and he wasn't shy about letting you know it. All three dogs had been anesthetized, intubated, and draped, the area to be operated on ready to be shaved and painted with Betadine, so the main grunt work was done by the time the students walked in the door—all they had to do was try to avoid slashing themselves with their scalpels and doing irreparable harm to their patients. The effect was that you really didn't see the dog, not in a holistic way, but only as a square of cutaneous membrane, under which lay the internal organs. That made it easier, and he supposed the administration had contrived it that way so as to eliminate any possibility of attachment to an animal that was destined, after four weeks and four procedures, to give up its being to a higher cause.

On the first day, he'd felt absolutely nothing beyond the usual fatigue. His breakfast consisted of a bowl of the sugary granola he'd bought at the health food co-op and as much coffee as he could get down in the twenty minutes he budgeted for showering, shaving, eating, and caffeinating before running for the 5:00 a.m. bus and starting his rounds at the hospital. Dog Lab met on Wednesdays, 8:00 to 11:00 a.m., and when he humped down the concrete steps to the basement, it was just in time to see Lurch and the other tech sidling out of the room after delivering the prepped dogs. They didn't nod to him and he didn't nod to them. That was the way it was—they were the working class and he the over-educated and underqualified med student for whom this was just one step on the ladder to something a whole lot better, or at least that was the way they saw it, and the way they saw it set him on edge enough to fit right into the role.

The first day's procedure was to make a midline abdominal incision, wait till Markowitz inspected it, then disinfect it and sew it back up. Jackson was surprised to see that there was no autoclave for sterilizing the instruments, just a dishwasher, but then if an infection should crop up, it wasn't all that momentous, given the end result of all this—and, presumably, the students could gain experience in treating the infection, in any case. Sipper, who'd been chosen to do the surgery while Jerry assisted and he cleaned the incision and stitched it up, even made a joke about it. "Not exactly the most sanitary OR I've ever been in, but then we really don't have to worry about saving lives here, do we?"

"No," he said, nodding in agreement, or at least in acknowl-edgment, "but if we're gloved and masked and following procedure, you'd think they'd spring for an autoclave, right?"

Sipper's eyes, isolated in the slit of flesh between mask and cap, jumped with amusement. "Dream on," he said, and somehow—maybe it was the coffee or the fact that he had unresolved issues with all this—Jackson heard himself say, "Yeah, well, somebody's got to say it, right? Or else we might as well be working behind the meat counter at the A&P."

Dr. Markowitz, who was leaning in to inspect the work of the group closest to them, glanced up at the tone of his voice. Jerry said, "You're right, of course you're right—but, Jax, in the final analysis, it's just a dog."

Suddenly, he felt himself grinning, and all the tension evaporated in that instant. "What would Gertrude Stein say?"

"Oh, I don't know," Jerry said, and here came Markowitz to see what this was all about, because this wasn't playtime, gentlemen, was it? "A dog is a dog is a dog?"

The second week, he was chosen to do the surgery, which involved opening the dog's abdominal cavity, finding and identifying the gallbladder, and removing it, after which the dog would be sewn up—in this case by Sipper—put back in his cage, and given a week to heal before the next procedure. He was feeling as exhausted and compensatorily caffeinated as he'd been the week before, but when it came to it he was steady and precise and everything went off without a hitch. Dr. Markowitz, who leaned toward the critical side and doled out praise in an almost homeopathic way, inspected his work and said, "Good job," which was about as much as you could hope for.

Still, the praise felt good, and since the next day was his day off, he took Juliana out for pizza at the place around the corner from her apartment and they shared a bottle of Chianti while she told him about her day and he told her about his, without going into too much detail—what mattered in the telling was that he'd controlled his nerves, done a bang-up job, and received praise from a doctor who didn't dispense it lightly.

"What's a gallbladder do?" she asked, idly licking a strand of mozzarella from her upper lip. Roxy Music was on the jukebox with "Love Is the Drug," a tune he found hypnotic—when he had time to be hypnotized, that is.

"Stores bile and lets it out when you're digesting your food."

"But you can live without it, right?"

He shrugged, dropped his eyes to the pizza, and separated a slice. "Yeah, of course." He would have pointed out the obvious—*The dog's got to last four weeks*—but didn't want to get her going on that theme again, so he concentrated on easing his slice away from the body of the pizza with its tentacles of cheese intact. "My mother can testify to that. She had hers out when I was a kid, and for years it was in a jar of formalin on the bookcase, propping up her shelf of Updike."

Juliana made a face. "I don't know, but that's grotesque, isn't it?"

"Not especially. It's physiology, that's all. I used to love to shake up the jar and watch it float around in there, thinking, That thing was inside my mother—and there's one inside of me too. Inside of everybody."

"And the one you took out of the dog, is that in a jar too?"

He shook his head. After they'd examined it for pathology, it had gone into the bin for medical waste.

"What, you didn't think to bring it home for *my* bookcase? It's like a trophy, right?" He didn't like the way this was going, didn't like her tone or the way she was looking at him. Wasn't this supposed to be a celebration? Wasn't he supposed to be happy?

He just shrugged—again—and then he was eating.

Two nights later, he was on call and making the rounds of the patients he was overseeing, one of whom he'd stitched up himself after kidney surgery, when the image of the dog came into his head. If he was checking up on the human patients, then why not see how the canine ones were doing? He got himself a Sprite—no more caffeine; his nerves were in a jangle already—and went down the basement steps to the converted storage room where they kenneled the dogs. As soon as he turned the doorknob, they began to whine, and then he flicked on the light and the room jumped to life: the dogs, the cages, the bowls for food and water, a chart on the wall, a bucket, a broom, a mop. The cages were standard transport units, which were manageable yet gave the dogs sufficient room to turn around and change position if they were experiencing pain. For obvious reasons, the school favored medium-sized animals—they were easier to work with, especially when somebody (Lurch) had to haul them around after they were sedated.

Well, okay, here they were. The other two, mixed breeds with whiskery faces and flag-like tails, stopped whining the minute he came through the door. The looks they gave him were without expectation—they sank down over their front paws and gazed steadily at him, as if they saw him for what he was, a functionary of the system that locked them away in cages and made them hurt.

"Jesus," he murmured, "it's okay, good dogs, it's okay," and then he was bent over his dog's cage and his dog was licking his hand and he was rubbing its ears—or *his* ears, that is, and how could he not have even known the animal's sex? Was it really all that abstract? No, it wasn't. He was a dog, a living, sentient being, an individual, a male, and that made him present in a way he hadn't been three mornings ago when he was nothing more than a problem to be solved. That was the beginning of it, he supposed, that simple touch, the dog's hot, abrasive tongue exploring the back of his hand, and his fingers stroking the silk of his ears, a moment that wasn't disinterested or scientific but something else, something that felt very much like connectedness, like pity, like love.

The next night he brought treats for all three dogs, and when nobody was looking he put the beagle on a leash and walked him up the steps and out the door so the dog could feel the night air on his face, sniff at the bushes, lift his leg. The whole thing, beginning to end, was no more than the fifteen minutes he allotted himself for his break, but as he stood there in the middle of the darkened flowerbed, all the frenzy of activity—the ambulances, the ER, the silent procession of headlights endlessly entering and exiting the lot—seemed to exist in another dimension. His pulse slowed and he actually looked up and saw that there were stars in the sky.

Every night that week, he took his break in the basement, and every night he took his dog out for a sniff around the lawn and the flowerbeds, careful to stay in the shadows in case anyone should question him, though he'd already worked up an excuse along the lines of: they'd operated on this one and he was having urinary tract problems and since the techs had all gone home and there was nobody to oversee things, he'd taken it upon himself, et cetera. And wasn't he a good student? Wasn't he caring? Didn't he see to every least detail all by himself and without having to be told? He found himself calling the dog "Dog," which in this case made the generic specific and to that extent, it became a private joke between himself and the little animal, who never complained, even when he lifted his leg against the tug of the stitches in his abdomen. He wasn't self-pitying, like the other two, and when he did his business and scratched around in the rich loam of the flowerbed, he did it with a brisk efficiency and then looked up at Jackson as if to say, *All right, what next?*

*   *   *

When Wednesday came around, he woke before the alarm went off. He was feeling cored-out and vacant, as if he'd developed a touch of the flu, but after jumping in and out of the shower and gulping down his coffee and cereal, he realized that wasn't it at all—no, he was nervous. Not on his own account, as he'd been the week before—Jerry would be doing the cutting today, he'd be assisting, and Sipper would prep. He was nervous for the dog. For *Dog*. Any operation was a risk, and things could go wrong, radically wrong, but he kept telling himself it didn't matter because the dog was meant to be sacrificed in any case, wasn't that right? Wasn't that the way it was?

He did his morning rounds and at 8:00 a.m. he was in the lab, the dogs sedated, intubated, and hooked up to the machines, and the instruments gleaming from the dishwasher, and did they use a rinse aid to make them shine like that? Sure they did. They had to at least keep up the illusion that this was the real deal and that the outcome mattered to anyone. Markowitz was there already, hovering. There were brief greetings all around and then there was the intense silence of concentration as the three groups focused on the task at hand: opening up the abdominal cavity, resecting a loop of small intestine, waiting for Markowitz's inspection at each step, and then stitching up the incision. Markowitz called out the steps of the procedure, as usual, and all three groups operated in concert: prep the skin; make a midline abdominal incision; dissect down to the peritoneum; enter the abdominal cavity—*carefully*, so as not to perforate the bowel... Jerry worked confidently and well. There were no screw-ups. For whatever reason, maybe because he'd used up his quota of praise the previous week, all Markowitz said was "Fine. Now sew him up."

That night he brought a box of frozen lasagna over to Juliana's and they watched a made-for-TV movie that was idiotic but soothing because it was somebody else's idiocy for a change, almost as if it were a prescribed dose. He'd checked on Dog before he left the hospital and the patient was groggy still, but roused himself enough to give a dedicated lick or two to the hand presented to him, though he left his treat untouched.

"So we operated again today," he said during the commercial break, which featured a Dodge Ramcharger pulverizing a streambed in a tree-choked forest somewhere. "Jerry this time. He did a great job, very efficient and sure-handed, but for whatever reason Markowitz didn't praise him the way he praised me last time around... which I think means I'm going to be the one he picks to do the big one next week, the heart procedure?" He ended with a rising inflection, as if he were asking a question, which in a way he was.

She looked up from her plate. They were eating at the table, the TV turned around so it was facing them. "What do you want me to say: *That's nice?*" She picked up the spatula, cut a square of lasagna from the pan, and lifted it onto her plate. "It's not the same dog, is it? I mean, how can you—?"

"Yes, I told you—there are three dogs and each team gets their own one, beginning to end."

She didn't have anything to say to this. She chewed, staring into his eyes a moment as if she were about to say something more, but she didn't. On the TV screen, oversize tires flung ribbons of water at the banks of the stream.

"He's really a brave dog, you know that?" he said.

"Brave? What's brave about being strapped down on a table and getting, what, cut up by a bunch of med students?" Her mouth compacted. "He'd be brave if he bit you."

"You're not hearing me. I like him, I really do—I even named him…"

"What's the point?"

"I named him 'Dog.'"

"'Dog'?" Why don't you just name him 'Nothing'? Isn't that what he is, *nothing*? Trash for the incinerator?" That was when she got up from the table and went into the bedroom, slamming the door behind her. There was silence, into which the return of the movie fed itself, line by banal line. He felt bad, worse than bad—she'd made him feel like a criminal, as if he were the one who made up the rules, as if it were all on him. What was happening here went against everything they were trying to teach him, and he resisted giving in to it—where was his discipline, his detachment?

When she wouldn't come out to watch the rest of the

movie, he cleaned up and washed and dried the dishes himself, feeling resentful now—she wasn't going to chase him away. He was going to sink into her couch and watch the inevitable shoot-out at the end, whether she was in there brooding or not. A week from today Dog Lab would be over and they could forget about it and go back to the way things used to be, because he had enough hurdles to jump as it was without her digging into him all the time.

When he went to the refrigerator for a beer, he noticed that she'd torn a sheet of paper from her notebook and stuck it squarely in the middle of the door with four reinforced strips of Scotch tape, as if it was meant to last. She'd inscribed a quotation on it in her careful back-sloping script, attributed to an animal rights activist whose name was basically anathema in med school. "We have to speak up," it read, "on behalf of those who cannot speak for themselves."

The days ticked down, everything a blur, but no matter how crazy things got, he made time each night to visit the dog and make sure he got his walk out in the world of sounds and scents and lights that got up and moved across the horizon. One night a cat came stalking around the margin of the flowerbed and Dog growled and tugged at the leash, and another night, a girl hurrying by with her book bag stopped a moment to bend and pat his head. "He's cute," she said, straightening up and giving Jackson a smile. "What's his name?"

Then it was Wednesday. As he'd hoped and dreaded in equal measure, Markowitz picked him to do the procedure, a right auricle resection, which involved cutting the muscles between the ribs, and then, using rib retractors and longer instruments, removing a portion of the right auricle, after which the patient would be patched up and sent back to his cage for recovery. When Markowitz called his name, he was so wound up he almost jumped. The dog was prepped and ready to go, but this wasn't some generic lab specimen, not anymore, and the last thing he wanted was to inflict pain on him—more pain, unnecessary pain, since as far as anyone knew the dog's heart was getting along just fine as it was—but then he didn't want anybody else to do it either. If it had been Sipper—or even Jerry—he would have been screaming inside. But it wasn't Sipper and it wasn't Jerry—he was the one with the scalpel in his hand as Markowitz called out the steps, and he was the one who was going to have to make this as near to flawless as humanly possible.

When it was over, when the stitches were in and Markowitz had made his final inspection, he was so overwhelmed he could barely speak. Markowitz hadn't said *Good job*, but he'd smiled and patted him on the shoulder, and Jerry was right there for him, like a teammate when the winning basket swishes home at the final buzzer. He should have felt jubilant, but he didn't. He wasn't going to be a surgeon. He'd known that before he started the rotation, and if he'd told himself to keep an open mind, which was the whole point of experiencing each of the specialties in turn, it was closed now. Oh, he had the strength and the fine-motor skills, but did he have the heart for it? Even as he asked himself the question, he had to laugh—the dog had a resected right auricle, but he had nothing there but a gaping hole. That night, late, when he was on call, he went down to check on the dog and found him lying on his side, all but inert. The dog didn't raise his head, but when Jackson called softly to him, his tail began to thump, as if in absolution.

Over the course of the next week he visited the dog when he could—secretly, of course, because if any of the techs or his fellow students caught him, he'd be an object of derision, if not outright mockery. There was the ear rubbing, the patting, the delivery of treats—and not just for his dog but for the other two as well, and when Dog perked up toward the end of the week, the leash and the walk around the flowerbed ensued. What he was wondering—and was afraid to ask—was how long the dogs would be allowed to recover before the terminal procedure, which certainly wouldn't involve any more consideration or skill than would have been required in an abattoir. The thought depressed him. Every time he slipped down the stairs and opened the door, he expected to see the three cages standing empty, and it came to him that he just couldn't bear that, and whether it violated protocol or for that matter was flat-out illegal, he wasn't going to allow it to happen.

From the pay phone in the lobby, where he could be sure no one would overhear him, he called Juliana and asked her to pick him up in her car. Right away. Now.

"What's up?" she asked. "Is there some kind of problem?"

"You'll see," he said. "And don't pull in to the lot—just park around the corner on Elm, where the drugstore is?"

For the next month they switched off between keeping the dog at her apartment and his, but it was problematic, what with their schedules and the inescapable fact that both their leases specified, in bold letters, No Pets. The dog was well-behaved, as far as that went, housebroken by whoever had selected him as a puppy from a kennel or an ad in the paper and then given him up in circumstances that could only be guessed at: the move out of town, poverty, sickness, death. Or indifference. A dog was a responsibility, a burden, as he was beginning to discover despite his best intentions. The landlord got on his case and he took the dog to Juliana's till her landlord stormed up the stairs and threatened her with eviction. And though Dog was house-trained, the gallbladder removal meant that he was getting a continual drip of bile in his digestive tract, which tended to give him the runs. He was always apologetic about it because he was a good dog, the best, the dog whose life he himself had saved, but there it was, shit on the floor, night after night. So now came the true point of reorientation: What was he going to do? Put an ad in the paper? Take the dog to the pound and start the cycle all over again?

No one at the hospital said a word about the dog's disappearance—for Lurch, he supposed, it must have made things that much easier—but there was no way he could confide in anybody there, not even Jerry. He tried to talk it out with Juliana one night as they huddled over the cluttered Formica table in his kitchen, because there had to be some way around this, didn't there? They were eating tepid cheeseburgers she'd brought home from Burger King while Dog waited stoically for the scraps, and the record on the stereo channeled the heartbreak of the blues. "I don't know," she said, "but I can't take him, that's for sure. Billy, my landlord? He just about goes through the roof every time I bring him over—you know that." She took a delicate bite of the burger, working her teeth like precision instruments to separate a piece for the dog, then leaned over to feed him from the cupped palm of her hand. When she straightened up, she said, "What about your mother?"

His mother lived four hundred miles away, in the town on the Hudson where he'd been raised. She'd retired the year before, just after his father died, and she was all by herself in that three-bedroom tract house with the fenced-in yard and big, rolling emerald lawn. He could have been a better son, could have called more often or even visited once in a while, but his life was hectic and it was difficult, increasingly difficult, and she had to understand that. And she did, he was sure she did. She was his mother, wasn't she?

"Yeah," he said, "I'll bet she's lonely, I mean, since my father died," and he bent down to where the dog was gazing up at him expectantly. "And what about you? Could you go for a little country living? Huh, boy? Huh? Does that sound good?"

He didn't call ahead. "We'll surprise her," he said. Juliana drove. They spent two days with his mother, who, the minute they walked through the door with the dog, knew exactly what was coming. "'Dog'?" she said. "That's no kind of name. Come on, Jax, you can do better than that, can't you?"

She named him Freddie, and when he died of natural causes, fifteen years later, she wept for him.

THE WORLD
OF INTERIORS

by HERNAN DIAZ

THEY WERE SINGING ALONG to "Octopus's Garden," bobbing their heads to the music and staring at the patriotic stickers on the car ahead, when Wendy turned around to find that Dylan, their five-year-old son, had fallen asleep.

"He's out," she whispered to her husband and turned off the stereo.

A sharp silence cut the car in two. Wendy looked out her side window; Sean stepped on the gas and passed the patriotic car. The woman driving it must have felt Wendy's stare, since she turned to exchange a glance. Wendy saw herself reflected in the woman's mirrored sunglasses.

*   *   *

Sean had rented a small cottage by the sea with money they didn't have. He had found it while procrastinating online. It was an unbelievable deal, he said, and they needed to get out of the city for a few days. At this point, he argued, adding a bit more to their considerable debt wouldn't really matter. Wendy disagreed; a fight ensued. But Sean had already put down his credit card.

They had met in graduate school, where both studied graphic design. As they made their way in their careers, it became clear that they embodied opposite ends of the profession's spectrum: Sean viewed design as an art form, while Wendy was interested in branding. Their combined income as freelancers had afforded them a more or less comfortable life, but work had slowed down year after year—a decline that had started, fatefully, with Dylan's birth.

Except for the few times Sean asked Wendy to change some settings on the unfamiliar controls of the car he had rented that morning, they didn't speak till they arrived.

Because she had refused to look at the pictures of the place Sean had tried to show her, Wendy couldn't repress an expression of wonder when they pulled up. Everything—the perfectly chipped paint on the facade, the mismatched chairs on the porch, the discreetly noble furniture waving behind the lead glass windows—had achieved the pale glow of age that so many decorators try to force on new things. Nothing felt calculated or curated. It was a simple, softly rustic house that someone had loved for decades. Next to it, a twin cottage, partially shielded by untamed briars, hawthorns, and thistles, looked just as charming. They got out of the car and hugged, smiling, in front of the house.

As they were about to wake Dylan, a car drove up to the other cottage. The couple that came out of it did exactly what Sean and Wendy had done: as if in a delayed mirror image, they looked around, taking in the lovely house and garden, and hugged. When the man reached into the car to unbuckle the child in the back, he and his wife noticed them and waved, smiling widely. They waved back.

The whole family spent the day splashing in the surf and having illicit snacks. In the evening, they grilled hot dogs and stayed up well past Dylan's bedtime to show him the stars he was unable to see in the city. After putting their child to sleep, Sean and Wendy had sex for the first time in months.

The following morning, after pancakes, they went to the beach. Wendy ran ahead with Dylan, who wanted to build a maze for his action figures, and they set to work on a strip of wet sand. After digging for a short while, Wendy turned around, looking for Sean. She found he was still back by the dune on which they had scalded their feet. He was talking to a couple. The woman wore a white kaftan; the man was in a sailor-striped hoodie. A little girl, moaning, emerged from behind the woman. The burning sand made them shift from one foot to the other, but they seemed unable to interrupt their conversation, despite the girl's complaints. The unknown man, his face hidden in the hood's darkness, picked the girl up, and the whining ceased. Wendy raised her hand as a visor to better see the group, disfigured by the glare, when, led by Sean, they all started walking toward her.

"Wendy, hi," said the woman when she was a few steps away.

Even though Wendy smiled, the surprised curve of her eyebrows made a slight detour through annoyance.

"I'm sorry," Wendy faltered.

"Don't be. We've never met. Unless you count yesterday. The driveway? We arrived at the same time."

"Oh. Yes. Right. Sorry. I'm Wendy." She extended her hand with what had become an untainted smile.

"And you must be Dylan," said the man in the hoodie. "Hi, bud! Cool moat. I'm Ethan. And this," he said, putting the girl down, "is Lou. She's five, like you."

The children started playing while the adults talked. How perfect were those cottages? How lucky had they been to find them online? How would they ever be able to leave? While they spoke, Ethan's toes kept burrowing into the sand, groping for moisture while he arranged his hood to better shadow his face. They made plans for lunch, and Lou borrowed a spade from Dylan before walking away with her parents.

"What's her name?" Wendy asked Sean once they were out of earshot.

"What? Who?"

"She never told me her name."

"Emily, Ethan, and Lou," Sean said, pointing to the spots where each of them had stood. "Aren't they great?"

They all had lunch at a little sandwich shop with picnic tables. Ethan had brought a cooler with wines from obscure appellations.

"Mom, can I have a Sprite?" Lou asked.

"Hmm." Emily pretended to consider the request in all its dimensions, looking up at the sky, her index finger to her chin. "Sure! Vacation!"

"Can I have a Sprite too?" asked Dylan.

"You don't even know what a Sprite is!" Wendy replied, laughing.

"But I want one."

"Sweetie, you know we don't have sodas."

"Oh, come on," Sean interjected. "Vacation!"

He gestured to Emily to stay put and headed to the register to get the sodas.

The children decided to eat under an oak tree a few steps away from the adults, who swirled their wine in their paper cups and gave tasting notes as a preliminary to real conversation. Later that day, looking back, Sean and Wendy agreed it had been a remarkable lunch. They hadn't even grazed the predictable topics—hometowns, jobs, parenting, TV shows—but had found themselves, at once, talking with lighthearted sincerity about rather intimate concerns and longings. Some of them confessed to hearing certain things from their spouse for the first time.

"Why can't all conversations be like that?" Sean wondered once they were back in their cottage. "I mean frank but not solemn. Fun but not snarky? And just with. Substance."

With that, Wendy got up to run Dylan a bath.

During the following couple of days, the two families got closer. When they weren't at the beach, they spent time in the shared garden, playing with the lawn-game sets they had found in a shed—croquet, badminton, bocce—and having esoteric wines from Ethan's inexhaustible supply. After lunch, they took the kids to get ice cream in a red wagon. Although they were reluctant to talk about their professional lives, during one of these walks, Ethan revealed that he composed music for films, and Emily offered a short, self-deprecating description of her research as a biologist. They didn't hide the fact that they lived mostly off Ethan's family money.

One drizzly afternoon, Sean and Ethan drove to the fish market to get seafood for dinner. Wendy and Dylan went over to Emily's cottage to play LEGOs. For some reason, Wendy always fell into the role of the guest rather than of the host. Even here, where she and Emily had virtually identical cottages, somehow it was clear that Wendy should be the one to come over. And although Emily was welcoming, a certain awkwardness in the air made Wendy create minor chores for herself, clean up after the kids, and struggle to keep the dwindling conversation alive, as if each lull were her responsibility. With dusk, Ethan and Sean returned, restoring a general sense of ease.

Everyone, including the children, helped make the bouillabaisse. Dylan, who had always refused to try shellfish, had two helpings and declared clams his new favorite food. Because the cooking took so long, by the time they finished eating, it was a couple of hours past Dylan's bedtime, but Wendy said nothing when Ethan set up a video projector in the living room to watch a Japanese animated film. The movie was labyrinthine and dreamlike. Every now and then, Lou asked a subtle, intelligent question, but otherwise she was enthralled. Wendy saw Sean nudge Ethan and nod toward Lou, whispering, "She's so amazing." Meanwhile, Dylan was confused, bored, and sleepy. He wanted to go home. Wendy left with him. Sean stayed behind.

The next morning, Wendy woke up next to Dylan, who was hugging a stuffed seal. She tiptoed into the living room, expecting to find Sean sleeping on the sofa, but it was still littered with toys and picture books from the day before. She pointlessly looked around while dialing his number. His phone went to voice mail. She waited for Dylan to wake up and, with the excuse of needing herbs from the garden, walked over with him to the neighboring cottage. While Dylan plucked some peppermint, Wendy peered into the house. In the twilight of the living room that looked so uncannily like her own (even some of the toys and picture books scattered on the floor were the same), she made out the shape of her husband, asleep on the sofa. Someone had covered him with a blanket.

Wendy quickly packed some food and told Dylan they were having a picnic on the beach, just the two of them. They played Frisbee and dominoes, bodyboarded and swam, ate fruit and read books. Sean called; she didn't pick up.

At midmorning, as she lay on a towel reading a magazine, she saw the familiar figure in the sailor-striped hoodie approach her from the dunes. She sat up, stiff with concern. He waved. It was only when he was a few steps away that Sean's face became visible in the shadowy cavern of the hood.

"I've been looking all over for you. I was worried," he said.

"I didn't want to wake you up. Or your friends."

"What do you mean 'my' friends? I called you."

"Sorry, I must have been in the water."

"And you could have called."

"I did." She put on a shirt.

"And you didn't leave a message? I mean."

Sean looked down, and it was unclear whether it was resentment or regret that furrowed his brow.

"I'm sorry," he said at last. "We finished the movie, and then Ethan showed me some of his work while Em put Lou to bed. We all stayed up super late. Sorry. Too much wine."

"It's okay. Let's just move on."

"I did say I'm sorry. I don't know what else I can do. I mean."

"It's okay."

Sean went for a swim with Dylan. Wendy put on her headphones and listened to a podcast in the shade. She drifted off, and just when she had fully fallen asleep, Sean woke her up. He was telling her something as he toweled his hair. She fumbled for her phone and paused the podcast.

"What?"

"I was just saying Ethan's music is amazing. Amazing. I mean what he does with sound. It feels. Like. Spatial. No, wait. Tactile. It's like you can *touch* it."

"Look, I've been on duty with Dylan since yesterday. I'm just going to listen to this thing now, okay?"

Wendy put her headphones back on and shut her eyes.

The sun had set, but a film of light clung palely to what refused to become the night sky. Ethan and Sean were grilling langoustines while Emily and Wendy set the table when a cry came from the other side of the garden. Lou was lying on the ground, weeping; Dylan looked down at her, holding a remote control and a car. The adults walked over.

"What happened?" Sean asked curtly. "What did you do to Lou?"

"She. It was my turn. She fell." Dylan's chin was already quivering.

"What happened," Sean stated, almost yelling. "What did you do to Lou."

"Sean, please," said Wendy in a final tone.

Emily helped Lou up and dusted her off. More than hurt or upset over whatever had happened with the toy and her fall, Lou looked frightened about the developing situation. Dylan's eyes were full of tears, but he was too terrified to shed them.

"I will ask you one last time, Dylan," Sean said with furious calm. "What. Happened."

"Hey, Sean, it's fine. No big deal," Ethan said in a conciliatory tone. "It's all good."

"Dylan." Sean was turning crimson. "What did you do to Lou."

"What's your problem?" Wendy cried as she picked up Dylan—who now was weeping silently, breathing in tiny hacked-up pieces of air—and walked back to their cottage.

While she calmed Dylan down and got him a bowl of ice cream, Wendy heard indistinct murmurs coming from the grill. It was mostly Sean speaking. She couldn't make out the words, but in the cadence of his voice and in the long, uninterrupted sentences, Wendy recognized one of her husband's rants. Every now and then, Emily or Ethan would footnote his tirade. By the time Dylan had finished his ice cream, the conversation outside had lightened. There was laughter. A cork popped. Glasses clinked.

Wendy waited up for Sean, who came back after midnight. She ignored his coldly casual greeting.

"If you ever terrorize Dylan like that again. If you ever side with someone else before knowing what happened. If you ever treat us like that." Wendy finished the sentence there.

"He attacked Lou."

"What did I just say?"

"Oh, so he gets to be a thug just because he's your son?"

"You didn't see what happened. Nobody did. But you know that's not the point."

"Really? So what is the point?"

"Who are these people? Did you know them from before?"

"What?"

"Why wouldn't Emily tell me her name? How did she suddenly become 'Em' to you?"

"This is insane."

"You've been undermining me, over and over again, just to please them. Just to *be* like them. Your sycophantic behavior makes me cringe. It's embarrassing."

"Excuse me?"

"And then you sleep over. You sleep over. Away from your family."

"This is insane."

"And then. And then." Wendy started crying out of sheer fury. "And then you attack our child to defend theirs. That's what you did. And then you have langoustines and wine and laughs."

"I can't be in the same room with you right now," Sean said as he turned to the door.

"Yes, that's right. Go to *Em* and Ethan and Lou. Just know this: we'll be gone in the morning."

Wendy didn't bother to pack. In the beamless light of dawn, she picked up her sleeping son, put him in the car seat, and drove off. When he woke up, she gave him a vague work-related excuse for their early return and said Sean would join them later.

The first day back in the city, Wendy made sure Dylan was distracted and had fun—a new scooter, playground, pizza. Exhausted from her sleepless night and the drive, she put Dylan to bed and fell asleep browsing through menus of movies.

Morning came, and Sean hadn't written or called. It was hot, and both Dylan and Wendy were still tired, so they stayed in, puttering around the apartment. Dylan was more talkative than usual, and they had particularly engaging conversations. That night, Wendy started a journal to record her son's most inspired remarks, something she had intended to do since he had spoken his first words.

They woke to cooler, almost autumnal weather and went to the Children's Museum. After a shopping spree at the neighborhood bookstore, they dined at their favorite sushi place and fell asleep together, watching cartoons.

And then it was the last day of the cottage rental.

Are you coming back today? Wendy texted that morning.

He responded at once.

No.

Wendy stared at that word.

Got up.

Sat down.

Got up as an email from Sean came in—a long letter he must have had ready:

This will be hard for you to understand. I'm moving in with Ethan, Emily, and Lou. The four of us have talked about it over the last few days, and we all feel this family is now complete. I know you know I

Wendy threw the phone on the bed, closed and massaged her eyes, opened them, and stared across the room, her gaze suspended just above Sean's pillow.

She stood there for a spell, abstracted, until a faint smile brought her back to life.

"Dylan?" she called. "Put on your shoes."

"Where are we going?"

"You'll see."

On their way out, she picked up the keys to the rental car.

Dylan skipped ahead, turning around every now and then to make sure his mother was looking at him. Between two of his backward glances, Wendy sprinted, overtook him, and surprised him with a burst of laughter.

The car still smelled of seaweed and sunscreen. There were pails of pebbles and pine cones on the sandy mats. And sticking out from under an unused kite, that striped hoodie. Wendy strapped Dylan into the car seat, playfully refusing to answer his questions about their destination. During the short drive, he was jittery with excitement under his fake frustration.

They parked, and when when they were a few steps away from their destination, she asked him to close his eyes. He covered his entire face with both hands, but when they opened the door, the barking and the smell rendered all his honest efforts futile. Dylan squealed and jumped in place when he realized they were at an animal shelter.

They never finished the tour. As soon as Dylan and Wendy met Andrew, a mustachioed terrier mutt, the search was over. After some paperwork, the three of them were back out on the street. Wendy smiled as she watched her son walking the dog with sweetly focused aplomb. They waited for her by the car.

"Let's just walk home," Wendy said. "I bet Andrew would like to stretch his legs."

Dylan loved the idea and jogged ahead, led by the dog.

Wendy stayed behind for a moment, opened the car door, tossed in the key, locked the door, shut it, and again sprinted to catch up with her son. Andrew barked before she could surprise him.

ORIGIN STORY

by CORINNA VALLIANATOS

ALABAMA

HOTEL ROOM WHERE THEY waited for a garage to order a
new clutch for his Honda. The clutch had gone out not even
halfway through their cross-country trip to Arizona, where she
lived and he was moving. One food-stained issue of *Harper's*
between them, football on TV. She escaped the room to walk
through the plant nursery behind the hotel, mounds of fune-
real dirt beneath black plastic sheeting. Savage cold. The
sound of oncoming traffic was her life so far, and the sound
of it receding was her life now. Cupping her hands to peer
into the greenhouses, saplings like blind white worms. She'd
always romanticized the wrong turn, the unknown road, the

forsaken place, but now that she'd found it she realized it was the imagining she'd loved. The sky was colorless, like a surface someone had worked to scrub out. Waffle House, syrup shining from its pitchers. Running across the highway to the garage. The creatureliness in her limbs, the car sitting there like a trussed animal. Photographs of dead deer thumbtacked to the wall, the mechanics raising cigarettes to silent faces. She was foreign to them, and, to be fair, they to her. Someone had not loved them once, and so they got very close to things, like suitors in camouflage, and delivered the shuddering final shot and bent over the body and touched it. They might've liked to kill her, too, wade with their hands down to her heart. It felt like that in the garage. That the men it contained contained themselves a violence that lay in wait for exactly her youth and impatience. She returned to the hotel. To the part of herself that would live in that room forever, is there to this day. Finally they were told the car was done, and he went to get it while she packed their things. They hooked the U-Haul to it and started off. As they accelerated up the on-ramp, the clutch broke again.

ARIZONA

Vine-scrolled back house. The bathroom was doorless, a tolerable inconvenience for two people newly in love. She hung from the doorframe a pink batik sheet patterned with elephants walking trunk to tail. They called out to each other as they showered. She biked their sheets to the laundromat, zigzagging around broken glass, watched the sheets tumble, biked home again. The thing was, the fucking thing was that beauty was all that mattered and she would never have enough of it, the world would hold it in reserve because she wanted it too much. She saw beauty in nature, in the mountains piercing the sky through the jellied light, but as for herself saw only a smudge, a waviness at the edges. They drove south to Bisbee and hiked up the mountain to the shrine at the top, a series of hollowed-out rocks whitewashed and painted with blue and green birds, beaks pointed to earth, feathers clutched to their bodies like soft, plummeting pine cones. The hollows were filled with votive candles, crosses, pictures of dead children, tinsel, plastic flowers, cherub statues, pinwheels. She assumed the children were dead. It would be wrong, would it not, if they were alive, to leave them there.

WISCONSIN

Second-story apartment in a three-story house. They moved to Madison because they had a friend there. The friend wasn't a close friend—he had the potential to be one, but they didn't know him all that well. When they arrived they found that his life was already full, that they would be his thirtieth friend while he would be their first. He had a wife who made pie crust from scratch, an office in his house with glass-fronted bookcases and a crystal decanter of whiskey on a silver tray.

Their friend was playing the role of writer more thoroughly than she'd imagined possible. It both made her jealous and filled her with contempt. She thought writing came from seeing, and seeing came from never being seen yourself. She remembered everyone she'd ever met. The scabs at the corner of second-grade Veronica's mouth. The bright red iodine on her knees. She could go on, remembering. It was easy. There was something lazy about it. It asked nothing of you but your stillness. For you to light a candle and see where its smoke went. One night, at a bar with bewitching little tea lights on the tables, it seemed they had arrived, that the words could come pouring out of their mouths, that they could claim and wonder and parry and rise the next morning and drink a clear glass of water and get to work. But they fought. She felt for the car keys in her pocket and wavered upward from the table. Lights everywhere like a field of low-blown stars. But she went the wrong way, toward the bathrooms instead of the door, and had to turn around and walk by him again. He reached out and stopped her, and they were instantly reconciled.

FLORIDA

Old carriage house. They were teaching at a community college, but she had a breakdown and left midsemester. She found work as a theater usher, read *Paris Review* interviews on a silk sofa in the ladies' room lounge while latecomers inched down the aisles unaccompanied. She was no Charon, no dark-river guide. She was a gatherer of the small things one needed in life. She drove to the mall to buy pillows. He stayed home and took a nap. While he was sleeping, a man broke a window of the carriage house, smoked a cigarette on the couch, climbed the stairs, and came into the bedroom. He woke up. The man ran. She was driving home listening to *Tigermilk* on the tape player. It was winter. Is it more accurate to describe winter in Florida, or Florida in winter? One occupies, and the other, radiantly strange, is occupied. The moon was a frozen pond, its surface scratched by the claws of birds. She went to work at the seven o'clock performance. One of his friends came over. They built a fire in the outdoor fireplace and smashed beer bottles into its mouth and watched the glass melt. Suddenly flames came leaping out, licking up the wooden sides of the house, sparks drifting, lifting, rising with the ragged motion of mosquitoes to the roof while in the theater snow fell, a glittering mass that the stagehands would sweep into mounds with long brown-bristled brooms to use again. It was the Christmas musical. She heard the bells and singing through the walls.

WASHINGTON, D.C.

Basement apartment of a row house. The owner was never at home. He gave them a key to the upstairs and it was a good thing he did, for one day there appeared a ballooning in their kitchen ceiling, an udder of plaster leaking water.

They positioned a bucket beneath it, went upstairs, and discovered that the source of the leak was his freezer, a cave of melting permafrost with one white piece of wedding cake inside. His refrigerator had come unplugged. They called him and told him what was happening, and while he summoned a plumber they wandered around his living room, looking at diplomas in silver frames, Yale, UPenn, a class ring suspended in a glass cube. Years before, she'd mailed her high school boyfriend's class ring back to him in a padded envelope. Browned masking tape wound around the band to make it fit. They had been conventional together. They had eaten popcorn shrimp together. He had moved his mouth over her carefully, like a metal detector over a field. Now the plumber arrived. Not long after that, the row house was sold to a newly married couple, young but older than they were, already successful, prosperous. The woman had a baby. The baby's cries came through the roof. One night the baby cried for a long time, piteous and raging and thin, and she knew they weren't answering the cries deliberately, that that was what they thought they had to do.

OHIO

Split-level in Yellow Springs. Her grandmother had died unexpectedly, and they moved into her house, where they could live rent-free for a year. There was a grapefruit still in a bowl on the dining room table. She watched as it grew smaller and smaller and its pink blush dimmed, as it turned from an object of the ordinary world into a symbol, a locus of meaning, and she realized this was how religion worked, not to eternalize humans but the things they had touched, the places they had been, to make sure there was reverence and permanence in a world so porous you might fall through its cracks at any moment. Eventually, she tossed the grapefruit into the trash. They got married in a courthouse in Xenia with matching platinum rings they bought at Rita Caz. She wore a thrift store dress of red-and-white zigzags, he a pale green leisure suit with a sharp collar. Her hair was cut very short. The judge asked if they were in the military. Afterward, they ate soup for dinner, and while he built a fire she went into the backyard with the canvas sling to get more wood. She felt so happy picking the pieces off the stack. A staggering abundance laid out for her like this.

IOWA

Plum-shingled cottage with a baby in it. Snow on the side-walks, snow on the steps, snow in diamond treads in the entryway briefly before melting. Lollipop-colored light from the stained-glass window. She read *In Cold Blood* next to the baby with a booklight shaped like a glass page—you laid it over the page you were reading and the words glowed with a sort of docility. The hushed room, the baby's breathing. She had to fight to stay awake and sometimes she lost the fight and a wooly haze enveloped her like a plane passing through clouds. The morning after the tornado struck, they strapped the baby into the bike seat and took a tour of the damage, the sorority house whose roof and south wall had been sheared clean off, the rooms with their posters and pink bedspreads exposed. They stopped at a café, everyone being extra courteous to everyone else, handing out water, speaking cheerfully. They had escaped death, and though they knew it was blind luck they also felt a little special for it. Saved for *some* reason— for being nice, perhaps! Later, this café became the place she would go when she could get away. She'd order coffee and cake and stare at the screen of her laptop. Freedom wasn't to be found in words but in being alone, sitting by herself, thinking thoughts that would not appear in her stories because they were shameful in their intimacy and small in scope, the product of a lack of imagination or will or knowledge or something methodical that gave rise to what men wrote.

PENNSYLVANIA

Bungalow beside a battlefield. Eighteen-wheelers wheezed past the house at 5:00 a.m. Their son was friends with the son of the man who had hired him to teach at the college for the year. The man was the something at the college, and he was the something else. The boys attended the same preschool, which met on the grounds of a shuttered putt-putt golf course. The children played in the abandoned windmills. The teacher wore the long skirts and flats of the indeterminately religious. There was a shag of tall grass at the field's edge, into which their cat disappeared. She wandered its periphery, calling for her. The second day of the cat's absence, she knocked at the door of a neighbor who was reputed to keep raccoon traps. The man wavered at the threshold, eyes beady as a bird's, not quite believing that she wanted to come in. She did. She wanted to see. Stacks of newspapers. A tilting, feral light. The traps were empty. She turned to leave. The man was drunk. He opened his arms as if to say all of this could be hers, his heavy body, its broken kingdom. Who hasn't been confronted with collapse and wanted just for a moment to catch what's falling? And then to stay low, stay lost? She returned to the field and commenced calling again and this time the cat trotted out on her small paws, meowing, curling, her teeth hungry and white.

CALIFORNIA

Ranch in the Inland Empire, no Pacific Ocean, no beaches. He had a job on a campus of '70s-style buildings in the foothills of the San Bernardino Mountains. They bought a house thirty miles west. Freeways like the thick beige coils of firefighters' hoses. She wore a black velvet blazer to teach her class, pretending to know what she was saying. She knew enough to know she knew more than the others in the room, maybe. Or maybe not. That was the mystery. That was the mystery of being alive. You walked around unprotected. The winter rains came. In the mountains the rain was snow. In the valleys the snow was rain. There was no country here, only landscape. And cars like enormous cattle, cattle reared on blood and suet, roving and fat and free.

VERMONT

Vinyl-sided rental. Walking home after taking her son to school, parents biking past her, trailers empty of children, fleece blankets flapping over the sides like tablecloths pushed askew after a meal. Only one man ever said hello to her, a father who arrived on foot to collect his kid around the same time she did. He was younger than her but his son was the same age as her son. She invented a history for him, becoming a father in his early twenties, love and strife and separation, a minimalist kitchen, cologne bottle shaped like an art deco building. He was handsome, his hair close clipped, his expression firm. She turned away. Sometimes it seemed as if they'd moved to Burlington for the sole purpose of eating muffins and cinnamon bread. Dark at 4:00 p.m. Their neighbor's house strung with white lights in plastic milk jugs. Finally the winter was over and the last day of school arrived. She passed the young father shooting baskets on the playground court and stopped to watch. He made a high, arcing shot that swept perfectly through the net, and she let out an ecstatic cry, a sound so brazen it was as if someone else had made it. She wanted to show him she felt something reckless, that having been pent-up made her reckless because even now, in June, as a light rain fell, you were only a few months away from winter and all that secrecy and scuttling again.

CALIFORNIA

White stucco sugar cube. Life resumed much as it had before they left, though some people regarded their return with suspicion. They were teaching at a different college now. Small personal planes puttered at regular intervals over their heads. She gave a reading at the college and afterward a student said, "We were right there with you," and she realized that what she'd written was the desperate scrabbling of someone trying to tell a tale. But the tale would not be told that way. Finding the mints their son was using to mask the weed on his breath the day she slipped a ten from his wallet to tip the dispensary driver for her gummies. He wanted to be more awake. She wanted to be more asleep. A friend had a stroke, and when her friend felt able to see her again, she began going to her house to listen to her read from a simple children's book. Before they read they talked, and sometimes never got around to reading. One day her friend, with the use of a cane, went to the shelves near the fireplace and removed a thick black photo album that she opened to pictures of herself in a white bathing suit in Greece. Her friend was so young, but it was the quality of the *time* the photographs captured that made her cry. I don't know why I'm crying, she said to her friend. Later, she told him about it, how unashamedly she'd cried. They were walking along a path under a cluster of ash trees. They left the shade and moved into the sun and heard a crack and the shearing of something plummeting through brush, and turned back to see a branch lying across the path, jagged at the rip, the raw color of a newly sharpened pencil. They went to it and tried to lift it. As thick around as a marble torso, with that odd posture of a gesture interrupted. The flesh of the soul, she thought. They took a picture of it and texted it to their son.

The ground was no good.

Someone claimed sand would "do the trick" so we crossed the border and brought some back.

We put a thick layer of sand on top of the soil and planted new seedlings and watered them.

The water seeped into the sand and salt promptly rose to the surface and the seedlings died.

We removed the sand and salt and exposed the ground. Nothing had changed. One of us said he feared he was "going mad."

We began tasting the soil and discussing its flavor.

We agreed that some parts, those we had watered, were less salty than others. We therefore decided to dig and water the ground more.

Over time, the ground became less salty. We planted new seedlings, and this time they endured and then they grew inarguably big.

We fell asleep, satisfied.

When we woke up we found ourselves surrounded by a grand garden.

Satisfied, we fell into a deeper sleep, anticipating the arrival of ███.

We woke up late. ████ had already arrived but we found him on his back, long dead.

The sand we had brought from across the border had agents that were harmful to ███, we realized, and the man had died.

The garden continued to grow on its own, leaving us useless. Unsatisfied, we stayed awake. Our heads and hands fell off and we became stuck in the ground for good.

WILLIE THE
WEIRDO

by STEPHEN KING

WILLIE'S MOTHER AND FATHER thought their son was
strange, with his careful study of dead birds and his collections
of dead bugs and the way he might look at drifting clouds
for an hour or more, but only Roxie would say it out loud.
"Willie the Weirdo," she called him one night at the dinner
table while Willie was making (trying to, anyway) a clown
face in his mashed potatoes, with gravy for eyes. Willie was
ten. Roxie was twelve and getting breasts, of which she was
very proud. Except when Willie stared at them, which made
her feel creepy.

"Don't call him that," Mother said. She was Sharon.

"But it's true," Roxie said.

Father said, "I'm sure he gets enough of that at school."
He was Richard.

Sometimes—often—the family talked about Willie as if
he weren't there. The only exception was the old man at the
foot of the table.

"*Do* you get that at school?" Grandfather asked. He
rubbed a finger between his nose and upper lip, his habit
after asking a question (or answering one). Grandfather was
James. Ordinarily during family meals he was a silent man.
Partly because it was his nature and partly because eating had
become a chore. He was making slow work of his roast beef.
Most of his teeth were gone.

"I don't know," Willie said. "I guess sometimes." He was
studying his mashed potatoes. The clown was now grinning
a shiny brown grin.

Sharon and Roxie cleaned up after dinner. Roxie enjoyed
doing the dishes with her mother. It was a sexist division of
labor to be sure, but they could have undisturbed conversations about important matters. Such as Willie.

Roxie said, "He *is* weird. Admit it. That's why he's in the
Remedial."

Sharon looked around to make sure they were alone.
Richard had gone for a walk and Willie had retired to
Grandfather's room with the man Richard sometimes called
the old boy and sometimes *the roomer*. Never *Dad* or *my father*.

"Willie isn't like other boys," Sharon said, "but we love
him anyway. Don't we?"

Sunday-sized newspaper issues, sweaty human head issues, Z-shaped double books, magnetically bound triple books, books disguised as party balloons.

McSweeney's has taken a head-spinning variety of forms over the past twenty odd (*sic*) years, and we're just getting started.

SUBSCRIBE TO McSWEENEY'S QUARTERLY

Four issues of the most groundbreaking writing and art we can find,
packaged in the most surprising ways we can think of—for $95.

☐ 4 ISSUES: $95

To subscribe, fill out this card and mail it to:

McSWEENEY'S SUBSCRIPTION DEPT.
849 VALENCIA STREET
SAN FRANCISCO, CA 94110

Or, navigate to McSWEENEYS.NET/SUBSCRIBE.

BILLING NAME: ....

BILLING ADDRESS: ....

CITY: ....

STATE: .... ZIP: ....

EMAIL: ....

PHONE #: ....

CC#: ....

EXPIRES: .... CVV: ....

☐ *Check here if billing and mailing address are the same.*

MAILING NAME: ....

MAILING ADDRESS: ....

CITY: ....

STATE: .... ZIP: ....

NOTES: ....

Please make checks payable to McSWEENEY'S. *International subscribers please add $42 for shipping.*

Roxie gave it some thought. "I guess I love him, but I don't exactly *like* him. He's got a bottle filled with dead fireflies in Grampa's room. He says he likes to watch them go out. *That's* weird. He should be in a book called *Serial Killers as Children.*"

"Don't you ever say that," Sharon told her. "He can be very sweet."

Roxie had never experienced what her mother called sweetness but thought it better not to say so. Besides, she was still thinking of the fireflies, their little lights going out one by one. "And Grampa watches right along with him. They're in there all the time, talking. Grampa doesn't talk to anyone else, hardly."

"Your grandfather has had a hard life."

"He's really not my grampa, anyway. Not by blood, I mean."

"He might as well be. Grampa James and Gramma Elise adopted your father when he was just a baby."

"Dad says Grampa hardly ever talked to him after Gramma Elise died. He says there were nights when they hardly said six words to each other. But since he came to live with us, he and Willie go in there and talk up a storm."

"It's good they have a connection," Sharon said, but she was frowning down at the soapy water. "It keeps your grandfather tethered to the world, I think. He's very old. Richard came to them late, when James and Elise were already in their fifties."

"I didn't think they let people that old adopt," Roxie said.

"I don't know," Mother said. She pulled the plug and the soapy water began to chuckle down the drain. There was a dishwasher, but it was broken, and Father—Richard—kept not getting it fixed. Money had been tight since Grandfather came to live with them, because he only had his pension to contribute and it wasn't very big. Also, Roxie knew, Mother and Father had already begun saving for her college education. Probably not for Willie's, though, with his being in the Remedial and all. He liked clouds, and dead birds, and dying fireflies, but he wasn't much of a scholar.

"I don't think Dad likes Grampa very much," Roxie said in a low voice.

Mother lowered hers even further, so it was hard to hear over the last few chuckles from the sink. "He doesn't. But, Rox?"

"What?"

"This is how families do. Remember that when you have one of your own."

Roxie never intended to have children, but if she did, and one of them turned out like Willie, she thought she'd be tempted to drive him into the deepest, darkest woods, let him out of the car, and just leave him there. Like a wicked stepmother in a fairy tale. She briefly wondered if that made *her* weird and decided it didn't. Once, she'd heard her father tell Mother that Willie's career might turn out to be bagging groceries at Kroger.

*   *   *

James Jonas Fiedler—a.k.a. Grandfather, a.k.a. Grampa, a.k.a. the old boy—joined them for meals, and sometimes he would sit on the back porch and smoke a cigarette (three a day), but mostly he stayed in the small back bedroom that had been Mother's study until last year. It was referred to as *his den* by Sharon, *his lair* by Richard. Sometimes he watched the little TV on top of his dresser (three channels, no cable). Mostly he either slept or sat quietly in one of the two wicker chairs, looking out the window.

But when Willie came in, Grampa would close the door and talk. Willie would listen, and when he asked questions Grampa would always answer them. Willie knew most of the answers were untruthful and he was aware that most of Grandfather's advice was bad advice—Willie was in the Remedial because it allowed him time to think about more important things, not because he was stupid—but Willie enjoyed the answers and advice just the same. If it was crazy, so much the better.

That night, while his mother and sister were discussing them in the kitchen, Willie asked Grandfather again—just to see if it jibed with earlier stories—what the weather had been like at Gettysburg.

Grandfather rubbed a finger beneath his nose, as if feeling for stubble, and ruminated. "Day one, cloudy and mid-seventies. Not bad. Day two, partly cloudy and eighty-one.

Still not bad. Day three, the day of Pickett's Charge, eighty-seven degrees with the sun beating down on us like a hammer. And remember, we were in wool uniforms."

The weather report matched. So far, so good. "Were you really there, Grampa?"

"Yes," said Grandfather with no hesitation. He passed his finger below his nose and above his lip, then began to pick his remaining teeth with a yellow fingernail, extracting a few filaments of roast beef. "And lived to tell the tale. Many did not. Want to know about the next day, July 4? People tend to forget that one because the battle was over." He didn't wait for Willie to answer. "Pouring rain, boot-sucking mud, men crying like babies. Lee on his horse—"

"Traveller."

"Yes, on Traveller. His back was to us. He had blood on his hat and on the seat of his britches. But not his blood. He was unwounded. That man was the devil."

Willie picked up the bottle on the windowsill (HEINZ RELISH on the fading label) and tilted it from side to side, enjoying the dry rustle of the dead fireflies. He imagined it was like the sound of the wind in graveyard grass on a hot July day.

"Tell me about the flag boy."

Grandfather passed his finger between his nose and lip. "You've heard that story twenty times."

"Just the ending. That's the part I like."

"He was twelve. Going up the hill beside me, Stars and

Bars flying high. The end of the pole was socked into a little tin cup on his belt. My mate Micah Leblanc made that cup. We were halfway up Cemetery Hill when the boy got hit spang in the throat."

"Tell about the blood!"

"His lips parted and blood squirted out between his teeth."

"And it gleamed—"

"That's right." The finger took a quick swipe beneath his nose, then returned to his teeth, where one pesky filament remained. "It gleamed like rubies in the sun."

"And you were really there."

"Oh yes. I was the one who picked up the Dixie flag when that boy went down. I carried it twenty more running steps before we were turned back, not a stone's throw from the rock wall the bluebellies were hiding behind. When we skedaddled, I carried it back down the hill again. Tried to step over the bodies, but I couldn't step over all of them because there were so many."

"Tell about the fat one."

Grandfather rubbed his cheek—*scritch*—then under his nose again—*scratch*. "When I stepped on his back, he farted."

Willie's face twisted in a silent laugh and he clutched himself. It's what he did when he was amused, and whenever Roxie observed that knotted face and self-hug, she *knew* he was weird.

"There!" Grampa said, and finally dislodged a long strand of beef. "Feed it to the fireflies."

He gave the strand to Willie, who dropped it on top of the dead fireflies in the Heinz jar. "Now tell me about Cleopatra."

"Which part?"

"The barge."

"Aha, the barge, is it?" Grandfather caressed his philtrum, this time with his fingernail—*scritch!* "Well, I don't mind. The Nile was so broad we could hardly see across it, but that day it was as smooth as a baby's belly. I had the rudder..."

Willie leaned forward, rapt.

On a day not long after the roast beef and the mashed potatoes that didn't make a very successful clown face, Willie was sitting on a curb after a rainstorm. He had missed the bus again, but that was all right. He was watching a dead mole in the gutter, waiting to see if the rushing water would wash it into a sewer grate. A couple of big boys came along, trading arm punches and various profane witticisms. They stopped when they saw Willie.

"Look at that kid huggin' himself," one said.

"Because no girl in her right mind ever would," said the other.

"It's the weirdo," said the first. "Check out those little pink eyes."

"And the haircut," said the second. "Looks like somebody scalped him. Hey, short bus kid!"

Willie stopped hugging himself and looked up at them.

"Your face looks suspiciously like my ass," said the first, and accepted a high five from his companion.

Willie looked back down at the dead mole. It was moving toward the sewer grate, but very slowly. He didn't believe it was going to make it. At least not unless it started raining again.

Number One kicked him in the hip and proposed beating him up.

"Let him alone," Number Two said. "I like his sister. She got a hot bod."

They went on their way. Willie waited until they were out of sight, then got up, pulled the damp seat of his pants away from his butt, and walked home. His mother and father were still at work. Roxie was somewhere, probably with one of her friends. Grampa was in his room, looking at a game show on his TV. When Willie came in, he snapped it off.

"You've got a bit of a hitch in your gitalong," Grampa said.

"What?"

"A limp, a limp. Let's go out on the back porch. I want to smoke. What happened to you?"

"Kid kicked me," Willie said. "I was watching a mole. It was dead. I wanted to see if it would go into the sewer or not."

"Did it?"

"No. Unless it did after I left, but I don't think so."

"Kicked you, did he?"

"Yes."

"Aha," Grampa said, and that closed the subject. They went out onto the porch. They sat down. Grampa lit a cigarette and coughed out the first drag in several puffs.

"Tell me about the volcano under Yellowstone," Willie proposed.

"Again?"

"Yes, please."

"Well, it's a big one. Maybe the biggest. And someday it's going to blow. It'll take the whole state of Wyoming when it does, plus some of Idaho and most of Montana."

"But that isn't all," Willie said.

"Not at all." Grampa smoked and coughed. "It'll throw a billion tons of ash into the atmosphere. The crops will die worldwide. *People* will die worldwide. The internet everyone is so proud of will go kerblooey."

"The ones who don't starve will choke to death," Willie said. His eyes were shining. He clutched his throat and went *grrrahh*. "It could be an extinction event, like what killed the dinosaurs. Only it would be *us* this time."

"Correct," Grandfather said. "That boy who kicked you won't be thinking about kicking anybody then. He'll be crying for his mommy."

"But his mommy will be dead."

"Correct," said Grandfather.

* * *

That winter, a disease in China that had been just another item Father watched on the nightly news turned into a plague that started killing people all over the world. Hospitals and morgues were overflowing. People in Europe were mostly staying inside, and when they went out they put on masks. Some people in America also put on masks, mostly if they were going to the supermarket. It wasn't as good as a massive volcanic eruption in Yellowstone National Park, but Willie thought it was pretty good. He kept track of the numbers on his phone. Schools were shut down early. Roxie cried because she was missing the end-of-year dance, but Willie didn't mind. You didn't get a dance at the end of the year when you were in the Remedial.

In March of that year, Grandfather began to cough a lot more, and sometimes he hacked up blood. Father took him to the doctor, where they had to sit in the parking lot until they were called, because of the virus that was killing people. Mother and Father were both pretty sure Grampa had the virus, probably brought into the house by Roxie or Willie. Kids didn't get sick, it seemed, or at least not *very* sick, but they could pass it on, and when old people caught it, they usually died. According to the news, in New York City the hospitals were using refrigerated trucks to store the bodies. Mostly the bodies of old people, like Grampa. Willie wondered what the insides of those trucks looked like. Were the dead people wrapped in sheets, or were they in body bags?

What if one of them was still alive but froze to death? Willie thought that would make a good TV show.

It turned out Grampa didn't have the virus. He had cancer. The doctor said it had started in his pancreas and then spread to his lungs. Mother told Roxie everything while they were doing dishes, and Roxie told Willie. Ordinarily she wouldn't have done that—what got said in the kitchen after supper stayed there—but Roxie couldn't wait to tell Willie the Weirdo that his beloved Grampa was circling the drain.

"Daddy asked if he should go in the hospital," she told Willie, "and the doctor said if you don't want him to die in two weeks instead of in six months or a year, take him home. The doctor said the hospital is a germ pit and everybody who works there has to dress like in a sci-fi movie. So that's why he's still here."

"Aha," Willie said.

Roxie elbowed him. "Aren't you sad? I mean, he's the only friend you've got, right? Unless you're friends with some of your fellow weirdos at that school. Which"—Roxie made a *wah-wah* trumpet sound—"is now closed, just like mine."

"What will happen when he can't go to the bathroom anymore?" Willie asked.

"Oh, he'll keep going to the bathroom until he dies. He'll just do it in bed. He'll have to wear *diapers*. Mom said they'd put him in hospice, only they can't afford it."

"Aha," Willie said.

"You should be *crying*," Roxie said. "You really are a fucking weirdo."

"Grampa was a cop in a place called Selma back in the olden days," Willie told her. "He beat on Black people. He said he didn't really want to, but he had to. Because orders is orders."

"Sure," Roxie said. "And back in the *really* olden days, he had pointy ears and shoes with curly toes and worked in Santa's workshop."

"Not true," Willie said. "Santa Claus isn't real."

Roxie clutched her head.

Grandfather didn't last a year, or six months, or even four. He went down fast. By the middle of that spring he was bedridden and wearing adult Pampers under a nightgown. Changing the Pampers was Sharon's job, of course.

When Willie offered to help if she showed him how, she looked at him as if he were crazy. "I don't see how you can even stand to be in there," she said, wrinkling her nose. She wore her mask when she went in to change his diapers or give him his little meals, which were now pureed in the blender. It wasn't the virus she was worried about, because he didn't have it. Just the smell. Which she called the stench.

Willie kind of liked the stench. He didn't *love* it—that would be going too far—but he did like it: that mixture of pee and Musterole and slowly decaying Grampa was interesting in the same way looking at dead birds was interesting, or watching a mole make its final journey down the gutter—a kind of slow-motion funeral.

Although there were two wicker chairs in Grampa's room, now only one of them got used. Willie would pull it up beside the bed and talk to Grandfather.

"How close are you now?" he asked one day.

"Pretty close," Grandfather said. He swiped a trembling finger under his nose. His finger was yellow now. His skin was yellow all over because he was suffering from something called jaundice as well as cancer.

"Does it hurt?"

"When I cough," Grampa said. His voice had grown low and harsh, like a dog's growl. "The pills are pretty good, but when I cough it feels like it's ripping me up."

"And when you cough you can taste your own shit," Willie said matter-of-factly.

"That's right."

"Are you sad?"

"Nope. All set."

Outside, Sharon and Roxie were in the garden, bent over, so all Willie could see was their sticking-up asses.

"When you die, will you know?"

"I will if I'm awake."

"What do you want your last thought to be?"

"Not sure. Maybe the flag boy at Gettysburg."

Willie was a little disappointed that it wouldn't be of him, but not too much. "Can I watch?"

"If you're here," Grampa said.

"Because I want to see it."

Grampa said nothing.

"Will there be a white light, do you think?"

Grampa massaged his upper lip as he considered the question. "Probably. It's a chemical reaction as the brain shuts down. People who think it's a door opening on some glorious afterlife are just fooling themselves."

"But there *is* an afterlife. Isn't there, Grampa?"

James Jonas Fiedler ran that long yellow finger along the scant skin beneath his nose again, then showed his few remaining teeth in a smile. "You'd be surprised."

One night a week later, Sharon served pork chops and told her family to enjoy them—"savor every bite" was how she put it. "There won't be any more chops for a while. Bacon, either. The pork processing plants in South Dakota are closing down. The price is going to go through the roof."

"*A Day No Pigs Would Die*!" Roxie exclaimed, cutting into her chop.

"What?" Father asked.

"It's a book. I did a book report on it. Got a B-plus." She popped a bite into her mouth and turned to Willie with a smile. "Read any good first-grade primers lately?"

"What's a primer?" Willie asked.

"Leave him alone," Mother said.

Father was on a birdhouse kick. A local gift shop took them on consignment and actually sold a few. After dinner he went out to his little garage workshop to build another one. Mother and Roxie went into the kitchen to do the dishes. Willie's job was clearing the table. When it was done, he went into Grampa's room. James Jonas Fiedler was now only a skeleton wearing skintight skin. Willie thought that if the bugs got into his coffin, they wouldn't find much to eat. The sickroom smell was still there, but the smell of decaying Grampa seemed to be almost gone.

Grampa raised a hand and beckoned Willie over. When Willie sat down beside the bed, Grampa beckoned him closer. "This is it," he whispered. "My big day."

Willie pulled his chair closer. He looked into Grampa's eyes. "What's it like?"

"Good," Grampa breathed. Willie wondered if he looked to Grampa like he was retreating and getting dim. He'd seen that in a movie once.

"Closer."

Willie couldn't pull his chair any closer, so he bent down almost close enough to kiss Grampa's withered lips. "I want to watch you go. I want to be the last thing you see."

"I want to watch you go," Grampa repeated. "I want to be the last thing you see."

His hand came up and grasped the nape of Willie's neck with surprising strength. His nails dug in. He pulled. "You want death? Get a mouthful."

A few minutes later Willie paused outside the kitchen door to listen. "We're taking him to the hospital tomorrow," Sharon said. She sounded on the verge of tears. "I don't care what it costs. I can't do this anymore."

Roxie murmured something sympathetic.

Willie went into the kitchen. "You won't have to take him to the hospital," he said. "He just died."

They turned to him, staring at him with identical expressions of shock and dawning hope.

Mother said, "Are you sure?"

"Yes," Willie said, and stroked the skin between his lip and nose with one finger.

From NORTHERN ELEGIES, #4
by ANNA AKHMATOVA

A translated version by Katie Farris and Ilya Kaminsky

As for memories, they have three parts—
the first is only yesterday
when laughter is still heard, but our cheeks
are wet—this part doesn't last long. Already
a different sun is over us; not far
is an empty house, walls are frozen in March and in
    August humid,
where spiders are dust and chairs are dust and doors,
photographs are transformed
into photographs, and people come to this house as to
    a cemetery,
and, back at home, they wash their hands, breathing,
not breathing. But the clock ticks, April
becomes April, the sky is sky,
cities change to cities, witnesses die,
there is no neighbor to cry with, no face to spit at.
And our dead slowly walk from us,
to our dead. Their
return to us would be terrifying.
We find we have forgotten
even the highway number that led to the lonely house,

and, choked with shame or anger, jump in the car and drive
    to it,
but all (as in our sleep) is different:
neighbors, chairs, walls, and no one sees us—
we're foreigners. We got off on the wrong highway exit
and now we stand here
and we realize that we could not contain
this past in our lungs, our hands,
it has become almost as foreign to us
as a deaf neighbor in the next apartment is foreign.
And yes, we would not recognize
our own dead husbands, mothers, wives, children; and those
whom God separated from us, got on
splendidly without us—all is for the better...

NEIGHBORHOOD
DOGS

by TAISIA KITAISKAIA

MOST OF THE DOGS in my neighborhood are unremarkable, uncharismatic. Many have the blank, selfish faces of people on a bus. Some, of course, are full of joy and curiosity. The corgi in the little sweater is going places, and she likes where she is now too. The German shepherd who accompanies the elderly woman is also a figure of interest, his raggedy hyena back mimicking the woman's kyphosis.

Predictably, golden retrievers are popular in the neighborhood. Because I grew up in an immigrant family, I have always considered goldens the classic American dog, easygoing and blond, the kind of dog you don't have to explain or worry about, the kind of dog you can take anywhere, and exactly the kind of dog my family would never have had. We always had wiry, dark terriers who were menaces to society, who barked and bit people and roamed the house in packs of four. They whined and wept, and bled and humped because my parents didn't believe in castration. They were loathed by park stewards for chasing down migratory birds, and they spent nights in dog jail. They issued puppies that stank up the house with feral nursery odors. They had psychological problems, they were afraid of corners and flies. One of them actually murdered her brother. They were, in a word, like us.

Most golden retrievers are kind, transcendent, like midwestern pastors. Even the stupid ones are endearing, yanking their owners toward flowers for smelling and peeing. But there is a golden down the street who watches me stiffly from the porch of an expensive house, with a face I've never seen on a dog: the face of a disapproving father.

In fact, he looks just like my childhood friend Luisa's father. The eyes too close together, the bridge of the nose perfect for a pair of condescending glasses. I used to sleep over at Luisa's house for days at a time, and on the weekends her father, a doctor, would sit in an overstuffed chair in their vast living room, reading the newspaper or some medical journal. I often think that I only began encountering numb, lifeless people as an adult, but this golden retriever reminds me that, actually, I've been having brushes with these terrible people from a young age.

Luisa's parents disliked me because my family was poor—by their standards, anyway. My parents worked at the university, and especially at the beginning of my papa's professorial career, we lived in a series of shabby houses. Shabby neighborhoods in the Pacific Northwest have a specific sodden feel to them, as if years of rain have soaked into all the couch cushions and if you pulled back the bedsheets, a long, gray cloud might be lying in wait. No matter where we moved, we always seemed to be a short walk from a cemetery, and my parents would take the dogs there in the evenings, dragging my sister and me along. My sister and I were aware of our collective creepiness: four pale immigrants walking their black dogs in a cemetery in the dark.

My parents don't remember our life that way. They were proud of the houses we lived in. They had grown up in Soviet apartments; here my sister and I had separate bedrooms. And they recall our depressed, lower-middle-class neighbors with humor rather than despair.

"Remember those twins who kept changing their names?" my papa says. The two girls, my age, claimed to have legally changed their names three times. They had been born Micky and Molly, had become Cassie and Chrissi, and were now Lorna and Lena.

"The first time they met you, they said, 'And what's your name? Oh, who cares!'" My papa laughs.

And Mama still remembers Achilles, a lively, unsupervised dachshund who flew through the curving streets that always reminded me of the whorls of a snail shell.

"Yeah, Achilles had some kind of lifelong project—what was it? Gathering pine cones? Like a little squirrel?" I say.

"No, it was birds," Mama says. "Always hunting birds! He got a few of them too."

One time I went over to Luisa's house wearing a new dress. It was a rare day when both Luisa's father and mother were around. The father was in his chair with his newspaper, and Luisa's mother, a Teutonic woman, was in the kitchen, clopping around in her clogs and rectangular beige dress (she had a fresh beige dress for each day), packing up boxes for the country club or whatever. Luisa's mother didn't cook—despite all their wealth, there was never any food in the house—but she did do a lot of gathering of mysterious items to be sold at auction or given away to charities.

Between the kitchen and the living room was a hallway with a huge gilt-framed mirror. Our house had small vanity mirrors and a cheap full-length from Target, but this was like a mirror from a British palace.

I was so entranced by my new dress that I didn't follow Luisa into her bedroom but stayed in front of the mirror, twirling and gazing at my image. Straight ahead, in profile, head over my shoulder: like I was in a glamour shoot.

I knew I was making a strange scene, that I had been looking in the mirror for way too long, but I couldn't stop.

At some point I could feel Luisa's parents lock eyes across the hall.

"Where is Luisa?" the mother asked me in a pinched

little voice. Luisa's parents avoided speaking to me whenever possible.

I shrugged, still twirling. Who knew where Luisa was? During our marathon sleepovers, we fell in and out of each other's company in that large, cold, echoey house.

Luisa's father put his newspaper down and watched me. He was forming a judgment of me, a diagnosis to be set in stone shortly. But even so—my dress was so bright, my skin so tan from the summer! Look: it was me!

The diagnosis arrived. Luisa's father and I looked at each other and I saw it: *You are a fool.*

Then Luisa's father raised his newspaper and I skittered off, down the main hall, past oil paintings and glass bowls full of glass fruit—even as a child, I could tell that the glass fruit was a metaphor—and hard gold tables that were painful to run into.

Years later, in the summer before high school and before my family left the Northwest altogether, Luisa had a party with our classmates on the patio, overlooking her grand, green lawn.

When we were younger, Luisa and I had played croquet on that lawn, the grass hot and prickly. I didn't understand the game and was bored instantly, but Luisa was bossy, and the broad beige steps leading back to the patio were as daunting as a museum's. During the rainy rest of that year, Luisa and I played Lewis and Clark out there—which meant filling a thermos with Campbell's soup we scavenged from the empty cupboards, putting on ponchos, and crawling into the hedges to mutter, "Yes, Lewis," and "I don't think so, Clark." We sipped our soup and got quite damp.

But at this party before high school, all that was behind us. We ate chips and flirted with the boys. I even sat in one of their laps.

Luisa's father came outside and settled into a chair not far from us, again with the newspaper.

"What is she doing on that boy's lap?" he asked Luisa. Not really a whisper.

The little fool, at it again.

In those early years, my sister met me at the bus stop and walked me home from school every weekday afternoon. Because we hated each other, she walked far ahead, so we weren't even within hearing distance. I watched her purposeful body strut up and down the snail hills. At the house, we microwaved baked potatoes and added pickles on the side, a kind of garnish, and ate on the floor in front of the TV. Our parents would come home after dark, tired from long days of teaching and working.

On the weekends, I had sleepovers with friends, at their houses or mine. But Luisa came over only once. When Luisa's mom dropped her off that sole time, she looked around in distaste: the four barking dogs, the rough gray carpet.

Despite her palpable revulsion, my parents greeted Luisa's mother cordially and did not feel ashamed. They knew the opinion of this woman didn't matter. My parents had made our life happen on their own, in a country where they couldn't rely on anyone else, and they liked what they had made: on the weekends we walked to a proper park and played games as a family with a big rubber ball. There is a photo of my papa with his arms open, about to run across the park toward my mama. At the time, they weren't much older than I am now.

But I felt the shame Luisa's mother wanted us to feel, despite knowing I did not want a family like theirs at all, their bowls of expensive glass fruit.

One Thanksgiving, after the feast, my family drove to the beach. It was a brown day with heavy winds. I brought my novel with me. The girl in the novel was learning about her family's history during the Holocaust, and the book was full of winds, too, and creaking brown doors, and pronouncements from the elders that sounded like wind, or so it seemed to me.

We got out and walked along the train tracks. My parents seemed unbothered by their hair whipping back and forth, and the dogs were happy. Only my sister and I, peevish, already American, balked and whimpered.

My parents moved with ease against the wind, and I could see but not hear them joking with each other, because I was so far behind. Our dogs tried to rally me and my sister, running over to us with huge pieces of kelp in their mouths and then running back to our parents. My sister and I limped along, keeping our distance.

It was hard to tell the water from the sky. Almost no one

else was on the beach; only a woman who looked young and girlish from the back, and then turned around to reveal a deeply wrinkled face.

Finally we got back into the car, drove through the snail streets, brown and gray with a storm that threatened but never arrived. I got into bed under the lilac curtains my mama had bought for me so lovingly, and read under the covers, holding the little book and its horrors in my hands, just as the bed held me and was not afraid.

It's easier now, isn't it? Like my parents, I can move against the wind; I can see the doctor father in the golden retriever, a classic American dog taking on a classic American face, that of a miserable father who didn't realize capitalism would get him in the end too. No one forces me to play croquet, and no one's Teutonic mother judges my house. Or at least, like my parents, I don't take note if they do—my house is full of cozy things that I like, and that's enough for me.

I feel no longing to be stuck in the car again, to be driven to a beach against my will, to live on a snail shell street and befriend deranged children named Lorna and Lena, to seek consolation in the neighborhood dachshund with a vivid inner life. I get to pick my own dog now, and she's neither a wiry terror nor a placid golden, but something else, quick and quiet and smooth.

I don't want to go back to childhood at all, but I do wish I could stop limping behind on that beach and catch up to my parents as they forge ahead, look into their young faces, in the prime of their lives and aware of it, determined not to miss it, finding ways to laugh and be at ease, in spite of everything. What would they say if I tapped them on their shoulders now, longing to know them as a peer?

One night my papa came home from work with a curious look on his face. My sister and I put away the scraps of our baked potatoes and watched as he sat down at the dining table to make a beautiful paper doll.

It was a Snegurochka, the fairy-tale snow maiden in an embroidered cloak. Papa cut the exquisite doll from thick white paper, and the little white triangles and circles snowed down on the dining table, just like in Snegurochka's winter world.

That night we went to some Russian family friends' house for tea. And when we arrived, my papa presented the gift to the little girl who lived there.

The girl barely noticed the doll, left it on a coffee table and played with her vulgar toys—bright plastic things.

I was enraged at this unworthy child. After his long day of work, my papa had been filled with the spirit and had made a toy from his imagination! Didn't the girl know that my papa could do anything, that a gift from him was sacred? He could draw, play, cook—but he rarely did, because he worked so hard.

After the girl abandoned the doll, I searched my papa's face for pain. I couldn't find it. Was he protected by some kind of wisdom? Or was his hurt simply hidden? Even now, I can't know. When I ask him about it, he's forgotten the whole thing.

VIPERIDAE

by VICTOR LADIS SCHULTZ

NONE OF THEM KNEW the reveler. There had been no time
for such questions: a farmer had seen a rattlesnake, a big one.
His wife had nearly stepped on it. Only by God's mercy was
the creature in a torpor. Perhaps it had recently fed. The farmer
told of its coiled bulk, how its head had risen forth, quite
dwarfing the upright woman. He could hear the rattle all the
way across his field. Then the beast had eased its head back
to earth, slithered ponderously off into the backland. A few
hours later the townsfolk gathered on the plaza, where they
were now. Their ejaculations did not sound like questions:

How big was it!

What direction did it take!

Why has God forsaken us!

In fact this last came from the farmer as he lay in the bed of his wain, broken leg elevated to reduce swelling on the counsel of his upright wife. He had suffered the injury while scrambling to needlessly rescue her.

Here among the gathered a debate sprang up over how to deal with the beast. Some wanted to dispatch a rider to the capital for help. Killing, they argued, was for soldiers. Others insisted that would take too long, they had to form up, strike out at once.

God has not given this trial to the governor, said the ecclesiastic. It is given to us alone.

Why must we kill the snake at all? asked the upright wife.

Folk looked at her queerly.

It was terrified, she continued. Poor brute wants part of neither man nor woman.

Let's fuck that snake right between the fangs! shouted the reveler.

Whispers went around: Whom was he with?

Rattler that size, spat a voice—it belonged to the wrestler—has enough juice in one bite to kill us all. It must die.

The ecclesiastic nodded as if the wrestler had quoted Scripture.

See to it, then, said the upright wife. I am innocent of its blood.

* * *

The hunting party's progress was slow. The only one who could track was the arthritic. He claimed to have killed a snake of some size in his youth, claimed indeed to have killed many things, but now he groaned softly each time he knelt to read the clay. The babble of the reveler did not help matters—his anecdotes and boasts, his conspiratorial asides. At no point in those first hours was it clear to whom he spoke. They were perhaps a league outside town when the reveler abruptly widened his stance, opened his pants, and began urinating distractedly onto the snake's track. The stream passed mere inches from the arthritic's nose, and this affront seemed to upset the wrestler a great deal.

The reveler landed without exclamation on the turf, his manhood flopping about stupidly. The look on his face did not suggest anger, exactly, as the wrestler ripped shreds from the reveler's own shirt to gag him and bind his hands.

Why not just send him back? asked the youth.

We are near on twilight, said the ecclesiastic. He would not make it before dark.

We need bodies, declared the wrestler. He'll make good bait.

As he spoke he was pouring out the remainder of the reveler's flask. The spirits mingled with the urine and sank into the earth.

After that the march became more tense. The cuckold whined about how the snake could be anywhere. The reveler in his bindings exhibited a stoicism that must have surprised them all and a clumsiness that must not have. The tinker tried to discuss the weather with the youth, who glared over and over again at the wrestler and finally muttered something in poisonous tones.

Say that again, demanded the wrestler.

Just like when we were children.

You are still a child. Mother was right about you.

Muscles don't make you God.

The wrestler smirked at this and the youth punched him hard. The blow landed on his chin but appeared not to pain the man, who initiated a hold of such intricate design it seemed sure to break the youth's arm and will. After a moment the gasping youth kneed him in the crotch and the wrestler vomited.

Once the wrestler had recovered, their trek resumed through dusty vale and over rock-strewn hill. The ecclesiastic walked between the brothers. The seven men's weapons were what one might expect so far from the city: axes, spades, mauls. The arthritic cradled a musket that had belonged to his father and looked more effective as bludgeon than firearm. He alluded mysteriously to the heirloom's romantic provenance. The wrestler of course needed no weapon.

The ecclesiastic had spoken true; daylight soon grew faint. The serpent's trail led them to what appeared in the distance as a mouth, man-sized, perhaps larger, a blight of deepest black in the wash of eventide. The arthritic looked for a long somber time at the mouth. They all looked for a long somber time at the mouth.

We should camp, said the arthritic. Wait him out.

Heads nodded almost indiscernibly.

My father's father worked this mine, the cuckold stated without cheer.

They made camp close enough to the adit that the snake could not emerge without being spotted, but far enough away that it could not lash out at them from the depths with fang and venom. The remains of the old mill lay somewhere beyond their firelight. The reveler's snoring sounded painful, a mortification of the flesh as penance for his conduct on the trail. On the edge of the firelight his face was a soft thing, slightly pitiable and therefore disarming. The glances that fell on him throughout the night held no hint of rancor.

Surely we can remove the gag now, said the ecclesiastic. It might suffocate him.

A pair of hands unbound the reveler.

You know what I've heard? said the tinker with exaggerated airiness. Where there is one, there are two. That's not true, is it?

For a long time no one spoke a word. Finally the arthritic shrugged, patted his musket.

The rattler I killed in '63 was solo. I believe he was solo.

You believe? You don't know?

Ah. There were stories. A story. This horse dealer I knew of—a friend's friend—claimed to see a big one nearby that same afternoon. Seven feet, he said, a monster, almost as big as mine. They had to be mates, he said. Said to my friend.

The tinker sat very still on the earth and his eyes sat very still in their sockets.

No one else ever saw it, the arthritic offered. Maybe she died of a broken heart.

How do you know your kill was the male?

This received no answer. The reveler snored. Later the cuckold pointed at the musket.

Does that thing work?

Her name is Filomena. She functions, have no doubt. Ten years since I shot her. Almost ten years. Her lock is cared for, her bore cleaned.

Why do you not shoot it? asked the youth.

Before the invasion my father was a man with no dreams. He was brought up by women. My grandmother used to tell him he was not permitted to become a singer. Perhaps too late she realized he had no trade. The mining company was gone. The family had no land. He subsisted for some years as a leech on his sister's husband. He admits this openly. Admitted it. They slept him in the storeroom, or—if he was drunk—in the tub in the yard, in what yard they had. In fact he was sleeping off such a bout when the invasion reached us. He told the story often but could never say whether he was woken by his own stenches or by the foreign shouts. Slurs and imperatives. He rubbed the film from his eyes only to see soldiers, three ghostboys, herding some villagers from their homes. A gun fired somewhere, a woman's voice cried somewhere. My father ducked below the lip of the tub. For mysterious reasons his pants were down. As he was fumbling with his belt a creak sounded across the yard: the door to his sister's house hung open. He approached almost politely. Inside, he interrupted a lone ghostboy who was rummaging through my aunt's kitchen. At the scuff of my father's shoe the man turned and fired his musket so fast I should never have been born; my father had no chance to take cover. Except that devil fired too fast: before my father could think, before his tongue could begin to form a syllable, the ball ricocheted off a stewpot and sank into the ghost's eye. He died before my father could even start shaking. When the shakes did come, he didn't know whether they were from the pulque or the near death. He claimed not to know, I should say. In any case, he took up the man's ammunition and weapon, then led a counterattack that saw my father singlehandedly kill another ten ghostboys with that same musket—this musket, Filomena—that had saved his life in the kitchen. He rescued his sister and brother-in-law. The village drove out the enemy squadron. They hailed him as a hero, he who until then had earned so much scorn. The next few years he spent slaughtering ghostboys with great distinction. Later the general gave my father his own field command, but he was not fit for such work. It was too slow, he once told me, too genteel. In battle other men were at his mercy, his and Filomena's. In command, she mostly collected dust. Eventually my father must have realized those days would never return. He was as he had been. He killed himself in '66. With Filomena, of course.

For a long time the crackle of the campfire was the only sound.

How long do we wait for this worm? the youth finally asked. If it doesn't come to us, do we not have to root it out?

Several answers came at once. The ecclesiastic reminded them he had parishioners to attend to, souls to shepherd; simultaneously the cuckold stated they had nothing but time. The tinker waffled: He had commissions back home, but what if the thing was hungry next time?

I'm ready to go in right now, came the wrestler's voice came from the darkness; he was on watch.

We can last for days, said the arthritic. Weeks, if we make supply runs. The adder will be much more dangerous in his lair than out here.

It was agreed then: their pursuit would now become a vigil, indefinite and, as the ecclesiastic had assured them at the outset, divinely directed. The decision seemed somehow to ease the strife among them; the reveler's snores smoothed into the tranquil respiration of the blessed.

Dawn had broken, but most of them were still asleep when the dust storm came. Even the ecclesiastic, assigned to stand the final watch, had nodded off. Only the reveler's epic slumber saved them, for he woke up so early and apparently so alert that he alone noticed the strengthening of the wind, the sudden dimming of the still-pink sun. His shouts roused his companions but were not voiced at his companions. Rather he squalled at the sky—Why us! he cried, What do we do now?—as the others fell back toward the safety of the adit. Finally he turned to the mine with something like recognition in his eyes. Then he turned to the titanic cliff of swirling silt bearing down on him. This oscillation he repeated once more before unaccountably breaking for the storm. It was the cuckold who ran after him, calling about a broken neck in this terrain. It was the cuckold who sprinted now with his hand outstretched as for a windblown love letter while the reveler barreled forth. At the end they were both screaming, elemental screams, screams so loud they must have originated in bone rather than lung, until without ceremony the dust swallowed them. The rest of the hunting party had made it into the mine and had seen it happen, they each heard it. They each heard the screams, and then they each heard only the wind in entire. The ecclesiastic thought it sounded as violent rapids must sound to a fish, and he crossed himself without seeing, for the thickening silt had blocked off any remaining light. The tinker felt flying sand, stray painful grains, abrade his skin and his airway. They all felt it.

Deeper, said a voice; it did not matter whose.

As the five men walked, their coughs echoed back to them sounding stripped and stony, geological. The wrestler asked without emotion whether anyone had thought to bring a goddamned light. Barely had his tongue finished forming the question when the arthritic's face appeared to them aglow and annoyed.

I've enough oil to last a night, not much more.

The storm was muted now; surely the dust could not reach them here. The youth cried very lightly, only three teardrops that he had no trouble concealing from the others in the penumbra. He did not know why; the two men might be fine. Then he remembered the snake. Better to fall blindly into a canyon than to be poured full of venom, he guessed. He gripped his ax the way he supposed a warrior grips an ax.

The ecclesiastic had begun a prayerful murmur for the cuckold's health when a sudden coughing back by the entrance silenced him. The passage filled with the sounds of men and relief. Even the wrestler felt himself smiling as the party doubled back to find the reveler sitting exhausted against the drift wall. The cuckold stood there, too, sucking air with a hissing sound, hands on knees. He'd hauled the reveler here bodily and now was straining to think of no people at all, not a single living human being; he focused on this sensation of being a hero, or at least a survivor. The reveler in his spent state seemed a dead man, but in truth he was unscathed. He experienced a sort of euphoria. The skin on his hand was cool to the touch when the wrestler helped him stand.

These boys have some balls after all. I'll be damned.

Glory to Christ! proclaimed the ecclesiastic.

They broke their fast in the dark. In the dark they drank from two flasks—one with water, one with fire. To the reveler they gave two drinks of the water and none of the other. For this they regarded themselves as greatly charitable. The tinker chewed as quietly as he could: he was listening for the faint rasp of a stealthy rattle. He asked in a near whisper whether they had a plan. No one heard him but the youth, who then repeated the question verbatim for all to hear, and all noted his precocity, his attention to task.

My grandfather spoke of crosscuts in the mine, said the cuckold. Offshoots. The creature could be anywhere.

Creatures.

Perhaps.

So perhaps the plan should remain the same, said the arthritic. We wait him out right here, in his den.

Too dark, said the wrestler. The drift is too wide. He may sneak past unseen, lantern or no.

We can form a wall, said the ecclesiastic. Position ourselves across the drift. The serpent would not escape us then.

It's a snake, Father, not a fattened calf.

It could work. Let us lie down head to foot. The serpent would have to crawl over one of us.

And the man he touched he would strike. And that man would die.

Enough, said the arthritic. We wait. He will not sneak, he will signal. It is their way. We wait.

No one answered this. No one said anything for a time. The ecclesiastic contemplated the pain the venom would make known to him as it roamed his veins. They were too deep now to hear the storm but somehow it registered—a vibration in the stone, a quality in the air. The sands yet blew, all knew it.

In this stormy quiet they were surprised to witness, far ahead, so far from daylight, a homey will-o'-the-wisp receding into the tunnel, its voice upraised in song:

At the ranch they corralled him,
more than three hundred men.
But he jumped through their ring,
led them on the chase again!

The reveler had a wonderful baritone, at once technical and emotive. Despite the cuckold's fear, his confusion, he couldn't help admiring the tones for a moment before the arthritic distracted him with a black oath in that black place.

It's my lantern. What is that idiot doing?

Drunk, said the tinker. My flask is gone too.

He was patting himself blindly though he knew he wouldn't find it. An argument sprang up over whether to chase the reveler but it was an ethical argument, anyone could see that. The tinker's focus was on bodies, not argumentation. His body could be pierced and so could a snake's. The stone inside a mountain was harder than that outside a mountain, he was learning. The smell of fear differed not at all from the smell of damp limestone.

The tinker and the ecclesiastic would remain, guard the exit. They did not dispute the assignment. The ecclesiastic knew it to be soft work but felt no shame. God had a design for all his creatures.

The other four set off. No more song, and now the light was gone; no one had marked the exact moment of its vanishing. They burrowed through the perfect dark like God's mind through the void in the time before time. The arthritic forgot his pain altogether. A hand, the cuckold's, rested fitfully on his shoulder but did not agitate him, for such were the burdens of leadership. The plan was to hew to the main drift. All harbored misgivings, but no one knew how many crosscuts intersected the drift. The cuckold believed there were no shafts.

No one will fall to his death, he had said.

He offered no assurances concerning other forms of death.

All four of them half ran while straining to listen. A man could hear his heart pounding hard as footfalls or his footsteps like the hardest of heartbeats, nothing else. Occasionally someone called out to the reveler. One voice appealed to reason:

You'll be killed!

Another appealed to camaraderie:

We will not leave you behind!

Another appealed to practicality:

We need that light!

Yet another appealed to his sense of humanity:

Think of your... your loved ones!

After this last call they were all surprised by the sound of glass breaking far off to their right. Then, slowly, came the fright. The men felt a tunnel open along that wall, a foreboding stygian vacancy that manifested variously in their minds as a brickwork arch, a rough vent, a sleek alien aperture, and a puncture wound. To their right, then, lay a most primitive dread, but they could sense on their skins the distance straight ahead, the main drift in all its vastness. And so down either enfeebling path no man dared another step.

Back nearer the entrance, the ecclesiastic took comfort in his faith while the tinker tried to take comfort in his adz. They heard the shouts, barely, but could not distinguish the words—they were too far, and the storm was too close still. Closer than the storm though and no quieter came the tinker's inhalations, as if by sucking hard enough he could take in all this darkness and bare finally the light beneath.

The mate, he said. The other. The other. The other.

Are you well, son?

The tinker couldn't understand this question, could no longer understand any question, and thus gave no answer save more gasping. The ecclesiastic offered a comforting hand and a puzzled psalm.

Far away from the tinker's breath, all four companions took the crosscut; the original plan was abandoned. A grim sensation ran through their bellies. They had considered splitting up, leaving a pair to guard the drift, but the reveler was this way and they were here for the reveler.

We'll retrieve him and hasten back, said the wrestler; he imagined the reveler rendered unconscious by a chokehold and slung over his shoulder like so much kill.

Do not move! called the arthritic blindly. Be calm! We will get you to safety.

The dark distorted time. The youth could not guess how long they walked. Surely no more than a minute, surely no more than five. He tried to count his steps but lost track at his first stumble. The stone felt large against his toe, perhaps the size of a human heart. It skittered off from the dark into the dark. Not long after, he heard the crunch of glass, kicked a shard. The shard too now skittered off from the dark into the dark.

Ah! Ay!

The reveler's emissions were more indignant than pained. He was sitting once again. He had glass in his leg. He was hungry. This he told them all.

The youth heard a sound like flesh striking flesh and then the arthritic told someone to get off the man. The path ran in only two directions but suddenly it felt so easy to get lost, to guess wrong. The arthritic spoke tightly:

I'm going to use one of these.

The match igniting looked to the youth like a firework exploding before revealing a scene wholly unfit for the grandeur of sky: the reveler reclined in a swath of glittering glass and the arthritic hunched without judgment over the man's thigh, which dispensed a rich crude blood. And then nothing. Blackness, nothing. A memory with all a memory's attendant risks. The invasion, the ghostboys, had come and gone before the youth existed; sometimes it felt like a fairy tale. Or it was the real and he the fay. The smell of the expired match overpowered his nostrils in the cramped stillness. A sound that might have been a life exiting a body or a life being saved came from the reveler's throat.

Damn. Big piece in here. We'll need the father, his tools.

Can he walk? You—can you walk?

No answer seemed forthcoming. The silence was stretching into something other than silence, perhaps loneliness, when suddenly the youth felt three matches pressed into his hand and the arthritic's voice next to his ear.

Run ahead, fetch the father. All speed. Use these if you must. Only if you must!

I go with him, the wrestler said in a tone he thought men had used with women and children since the time of Babel.

The other three were to follow as best they could; the arthritic and cuckold were not muscular men. Off ran the youth and the wrestler, off, in a lightlessness so complete it held for the cuckold a distinct texture, a grained rub against the skin reminiscent of the blanket he'd slept under as a boy. The touch of others was now strange, but the reveler's head lolled briefly and not without affection onto his shoulder. Dust had made them sentimental. The man was trying to walk but could accept no weight on his injured leg. He was unaccountably heavier than he'd been in the dust storm, despite the arthritic's help, despite the cuckold's heroism.

Far ahead, the youth slowed his brother as much as he dared. They could not risk traveling faster than at a trot. They might miss their turn, crash headlong into the far wall of the drift. They might misstep, break an ankle. They might bumble into the preying snake. He knew the wrestler would consider none of this, knew he thought himself invulnerable. Yesterday's vomiting would already be forgotten, expelled from the wrestler's mind as the digesta had been expelled from his body. A year from now, should any of them live another year, none of the party were likely to remember it. Why should they? And so the incident would exist only in the youth's head. It would in effect be a delusion—the weakness of the wrestler would exist only as an infinitesimal worm in the youth's brain. Perhaps the youth would someday tell the story to his own son, how Papa had once bested Uncle; the disease would be passed on. And something too—a charge or a code, a kind of skin phrase—passed now from the wrestler's hand into the youth's. Neither was oblivious to the thing, yet neither fully noticed it. Neither could have named it with his tongue, had he noticed, and so its name remained known only in their bones.

TK-TK. TK-TK-TK. TKTKTKTSKTSKTSKTSKTSK SKTSKTSKTSKTSKTSKTSKTSKTSKTSKTSKTSKTSKTSK! TK-TK-TK-TK-TK-TK-TK-TK. TK.

The youth took the first great tick that hit his ear to be an earthquake, some epochal event in the belly of the world. This could be no snake rattle before him, no mere expression of flesh, it was too loud, almost cyclonic in its ability to spin a cold paralysis into one's nerves and tongue. And yet here the wrestler set up between the youth and the horrible knell, a petty bilious human shield defending as he had since their infancies his sovereignty as the youth's sole tormenter. His elbows held the youth in place, his back smelled sweetly of spoiled meat. No one uttered a word, for the serpent's question was too ancient to answer.

Then, in purest jet, they heard the susurrant slide of scale across scale, smooth death unseeable. And, too, the creature's slow, protracted scuff against the dirt, almost a crackle, as if near them burned the world's largest wick. Sound here could not be adulterated; the youth noted a wetness in the wrestler's air passage and let fall his ax. Tool of man had no place here. Man himself had no place here. The flesh had always sensed it; only now knew the mind. They would be absorbed into the snake's being. They would in time be excreted through its hide in strange oils, they would be sloughed off with its skin and here left as a membranous monument. Against his boot he struck a match to look, just the once, upon what they would become.

The serpent lay too far away to see, or, rather, most of its body lay too far away, in the drift. Here in the crosscut, the thing's head seemed to float perhaps five feet in front of the wrestler, who did not at first recognize it as organic matter. His brain processed the head as an old mining implement, a kind of engine. Then it was an impossible stalagmite. It was the size of the rain barrels the wrestler used to haul two at a time to impress girls. Only a slight but mesmeric waver in the stalagmite's bearing gave it away. Its tongue flickered once, more snakelike than the snake itself, and suddenly the wrestler missed his mother terribly, her warmth. They had never been close when she was alive.

The faraway matchglow shone to the cuckold like the smoldering hearth in his love's home, spied through a window at distance. Scarcely had he seen the illumination before it disappeared, but the time was sufficient: sufficient to feel the reveler's weight double on his shoulder; sufficient to revisit fleetingly the better times, those temperate days; sufficient to distinguish, ominously in the depths, the head of the adder looking large enough from here to swallow the wrestler whole. Hope left the cuckold, and only as the feeling drained from his pores did he realize he'd still held any. Then, deafening, final, a thunderclap next to his ear.

Filomena fired in full dark. The arthritic heard not a thing, so hurried was he, so deep in concentration. She fired at a memory of where the snake's head had been, and her shot was true, he sensed it, blind but true, though truer still was the curious sense of falling he experienced in that instant, so like that spring solstice in his early years when his father's war friend had visited, his tall friend who so loved to dandle children on his knee. The arthritic was too young then to remember names. He recalled his father and the friend laughing, then cursing, then laughing again but much quieter. And he recalled the stopping, without warning, of the friend's heart. All that weight. The distance from knee to floor interminable. Of course his memory of the heartbeat ceasing had to be an invention. It had to be.

No toddling child could sense such a thing; the arthritic knew this.

He slammed the bayonet into place and it rang in his ears like a ricochet off a stewpot. He could not charge blindly so he picked his way forward—a bayonet creep. Ahead he could now hear the scuffing, the colossal wick burning down, and whispers that could have been voices or could have been the distant swish of the dust storm. Without warning a bulb of light burst forth: the youth's second match steadied the arthritic. In its glow the snake's throes were a thing of ritual, a ritual the men were sure they had seen before, though they had not. Lo! did the serpent offer its blood to the youth. In that moment it lived still, as did the men, even if their sudden remembrance of everything true and false was a kind of death, but in the next moment the arthritic followed bullet with blade. The bayonet slid into the creature's brain, and a hollow fang unfolded piteously, and it ran longer than the bayonet, and the men forgot. Some things they forgot.

The match guttered out. Much exultation commenced, first inwardly, then audibly. Their laughter grew louder than the rattle, louder than the long-ago clamor of industry herein. They reached for one another's shoulders with great feeling.

What was that thing? said the youth finally.

Twenty-one feet! called the wrestler. I paced it out. My arms just barely fit round its belly.

My god.

Is it even a snake?

It is the snake of snakes.

A shot for the ages, my friend.

The cuckold and the reveler, when they arrived at the intersection, received the welcome of long-lost friends. They offered congratulations because they did not know what else to offer. The reveler had never felt pain like this.

My leg, he complained.

They settled for the head, as this body was enough to crush them all. The blindness had a dampening effect on the youth's disgust: the trunk of the snake beneath his ax yielded much like the trunk of a mesquite he'd once taken down in their yard. It burned well, its story did not matter.

Soon after, the wrestler tried to ignore the refreshing cool of the scales against his skin. The serpent's head fit in his arms as he, taken by sleep, had once fit in his father's. The men filed up that benighted path to share the good news.

The cuckold could not at first puzzle out why he was hearing the prayer for the departed. The ecclesiastic's source-less voice held steady through the O Lords. It spoke of a life, and the cuckold thought with some bewilderment that it referred to the snake's life. Why pray for the beast? The voice held steady through the amen. Only when the reveler asked boorishly who had pissed in the Communion wine did the cuckold understand that the tinker had fallen.

The ecclesiastic chose to be kind.

It was the rattle, he said as he dressed the reveler's laceration. So loud. The poor man was already near mad with fear that the serpent had a mate. He began swinging the adz wildly, I could hear it. He collapsed simultaneous with the gunshot.

At that moment the youth lit his final match. He could not determine the color of blood on his ax. The tinker looked untroubled on his back and quite healthy in death. All his blood remained in his body. The ecclesiastic's face regarded the snake's with a revolted beatitude and then all went black.

He was so sure there was another, said the ecclesiastic before taking up a prayer of thanksgiving.

The tinker's body proved inconvenient, it is true. The wrestler was forced to surrender the head to the beast's slayer. He felt forced. Strength was a curse, he suspected. The suspicion did not last. The cuckold assisted him indelicately.

Watch his head, said a voice the cuckold couldn't identify.

The storm had passed; they could hear it, its absence. Up the drift lay home, up and out. The ecclesiastic walked behind the dead and those carrying the dead. He assumed the same solemn posture he had in his first cortege, decades ago. Behind him the youth assisted the injured man, or so the ecclesiastic presumed. He did not know the youth's offer had been refused, that the youth now walked alone, lost in his own thought. No one saw the reveler slither off.

THE LITTLE MEN

by CARL NAPOLITANO

THE NIGHT THE LITTLE men were born, Seamus and I were naked, swaying in his hammock in his secluded backyard. It was late summer—the season for overripe fruit, fairies, and fucking—and we had been out there for many hours, talking about his flower garden and my upcoming art show, kissing indulgently, taking turns inside each other. The air was humid and sticky but there was a breeze that goose-bumped our skin, so Seamus had started a fire to keep us warm. At this point, he was jerking me off slowly, and when I came, it shot over our heads in an arc so astounding, Brancusi would have wanted to cast it in bronze and polish it till it shone. My semen landed on the ground fifteen feet behind us and we had a great laugh about it. My hands were shaking. I pressed my smile into Seamus's bright red hairy chest.

It was Seamus who noticed the little men first, their small bodies wriggling up from the dirt. "What's that?" he asked, pointing as we sipped our wine. I couldn't see clearly in the dark and thought they were moles. Then I thought they were pixies, except pixies have wings and aren't native to the South. Seamus grabbed his phone, turned on the flashlight, and hurried toward them while I stood back and watched. In the small spotlight, I could see their bare skin bright against the dark soil as they unearthed themselves, gasping for air, pushing down with their tiny arms to free their tiny hips and legs. "They're so cute!" Seamus gushed, crouching over them. "They look just like you!"

I wanted to vomit, double over and empty all the wine and Seamus's cum from my stomach, but I held it in. "Come over here, Leo!" Seamus beckoned. He put his free hand on the ground, palm open, and one of the little men crawled onto it. Seamus stood, lifting the little man, while the other five, who had by now fully surfaced, jumped and squealed around his bare feet. He looked at me warmly and said, "Don't be shy. This is the most amazing thing I've ever seen."

And Seamus had seen many things. He was forty-six, twenty years older than me, and in his life he had not shied away from pleasure—especially the pleasures of men and their strangeness. And he was not shy in telling me about them either. There was the man with two perfectly functioning cocks side by side, like the Roman numeral II; the man with the velvet, prehensile tail he could use to jack off hands-free; the man who grew twisting goat horns whenever he got hard; the man who could retract his dick and his balls into his body and transform them into a warm and inviting vagina. But these little men who had sprouted from the ground were not an aberration of my body; they were newly created bodies.

It made me dizzy to look at the little man in Seamus's palm, lifted high into the air; he looked not frightened but elated and wide-eyed with wonder. Seamus came toward me, stepping over the others, and said, "Hold out your hand."

I obeyed. I was good at following orders, even kind ones. Seamus let the little man crawl down from his hand into mine, smaller and sweatier than his—and less steady. The little man's legs were still clumsy, like a newborn foal's. Of course, I dropped him.

I tried to catch him, but I wasn't quick enough. Seamus cried out. The little man screamed his high-pitched scream as he fell through the air, and I could already hear it—the crunch of bones, the mangle of his little body, limbs bent out of shape, and a little puddle of blood. I was crying when, with a soft thud, the little man landed in the dirt on all fours and rolled immediately—a full two feet—spreading out the force of impact, till he was lying on his back, breathing hard and entirely alive, completely intact. Seamus and I squealed with relief. The other little men rushed to their brother and hugged him and kissed him all over. They wailed with joy.

They lifted him to his feet. They held hands and spun around in a circle until they grew dizzy and fell onto their backs, giggling. I smiled and then I didn't.

What was I to do with them?

Seamus was certain: I had to take them home with me. I couldn't leave them at his house, even though it was much bigger than my one-bedroom apartment, on account of his three cats, who loved to hunt chipmunks and would no doubt kill the little men in a fit of play. Besides, they were mine, not his.

"But you had something to do with this," I said as he gathered them into a cardboard box. "This is partly your fault."

"This is nobody's fault," Seamus assured me. "This isn't some misfortune. Of course, I'll help, but you need to calm down, Leo. Freaking out won't help."

"I know that!" I snapped, then apologized.

Seamus hugged me and kissed me on the cheek. We both smelled like smoke, but only I felt like it inside, billowing, building, burning. "Yes," he said, "but sometimes you get nervous when you don't need to be. Remember the first time we met? When I got you naked? Your voice got so high. But look how good we are together. You'll be fine. I can tell."

He handed me the box, and there they were, the six of them, looking up at me with my round, stubbly face. I wondered if I looked like their god. I averted my gaze, looked at my own large hands instead.

On the drive home, I thought the worst. It was late by then, two or three in the morning. There were no other cars around and no one out. I rolled down the windows to let the night air in. The little men were sleeping soundly in the passenger seat, in their box. I pulled over on a bridge across the river and looked out at the water. It was dark and calm, winking with moonlight. I could hear the soft breathing of the little men beside me. Something heavy and jagged tore through my chest, but I let it pass. I drove home.

It was the next morning, a Sunday, when I woke and remembered the bewildering warning my mother had given me months before. I called her now, and she picked up the phone right away and said, "Leo! My son!" But her voice lowered and lost its verve when she heard my silence. "What's going on?"

"I didn't listen, Mom. I'm sorry. I forgot." I poked my head quietly into my bathroom, and the little men, no taller than four inches, were already awake, frolicking naked on the towel I'd laid out for them in my bathtub. They were curious and cute, like kittens, and I quickly shut the door, before they could notice me.

That past winter, when I was home for the holidays, my mother had walked in on me masturbating for the first time in my twenty-six years of life. I don't know why I forgot to lock the door and I don't know why she didn't knock. Whatever the reasons, it doesn't matter. As soon as she saw me, she immediately turned and shut the door, and I went red-faced and soft. For several seconds, the only sound I could hear was the thudding of my heart and the buzzing of the butt plug inside me.

When I went downstairs, I had found my mother in the kitchen, loading the aftermath of our dinner into the dishwasher. My father was in the living room, watching fútbol at full volume, and screaming at the TV in Spanish. For much of my childhood, he'd tried to get me to join him, but I could never get myself to care so much about something that I thought mattered so little. His team would lose and he'd spend the rest of the day muttering, glum and pissy. Or his team would win and he'd glow bright and sing like an angel. What was the point of all those feelings? It was just a game. And I couldn't understand him, anyway—I'd never learned to speak Spanish. He'd never taught me. My mother spoke only English. She watched me pour myself a glass of water.

"You know, honey, you shouldn't drink so much water before bed," she had said. "Remember how you used to wet the bed?"

"Mom, I can wake up to pee," I said, laughing awkwardly. "I'm not a child."

My mother looked me in the eye, her face strained. This wasn't the point she had wanted to make. She hesitated, then said, "Your father wanted me to tell you: don't let your semen touch the ground."

"What?" I said.

"Outside," she clarified, her voice quick and uncomfortable under the roar of the soccer game and my father's useless shouting. "The floor doesn't count. Concrete patios and wood porches are fine too, he says. It's the earth you have to worry about. Don't let it touch the dirt."

I'd nodded, mortified, so embarrassed by the statement, by having just been caught jerking off, that I hadn't asked her any questions. And she, also mortified, also embarrassed by the statement, by having just caught me jerking off, hadn't said more. Not before I ran away, back upstairs to my room.

And then I'd pushed it behind the curtains of my mind.

That Sunday morning on the phone, she said, "Oh, Leo. How many are there?"

"Six," I answered.

She was silent for a moment and said only "Oh, darling."

I felt a panic rising in me. "How did this happen? Why didn't you tell me *this* would happen?"

My mom sighed heavily. "I'm sorry. I should've told you everything your father told me to, but I... didn't know how. I didn't think you'd believe me." She was always taking the blame away from my father.

"That's not true, Mom." I pressed my back to the bathroom door, like a barricade. "When have I ever not believed you?"

"When you told me you liked boys and I told you I still loved you," she said, her voice hushed.

She didn't mention how after I told her, I had asked her not to tell my father, and she had said she wouldn't, but then she'd told him anyway. She didn't mention his subsequent freak-out, all the shouting I'd tried not to hear from my room.

How he had driven off for the entire night to god-knows-where. She didn't mention the weeks he spent not speaking a single word to me. Didn't mention the stilted way he had regarded me from then on. Perhaps my mother was right: perhaps I wouldn't have believed her after that.

But she shouldn't have been the one to have to tell me.

These little men were a family thing, my mother explained now, from my father's father. My grandfather, he was from Colombia. He had immigrated here, met a Spanish woman, and had a family. He died of colon cancer years before I was born. Most of my father's extended family still lived in Colombia, and I'd never met them either. When I asked my mother what they would do with the little men, hoping for an out, she told me in a whisper: "They leave them in the jungle. For the animals to eat."

Then I asked, "Has this happened to Dad? What did he do?"

"You know, honey, I don't know. He didn't tell me. You know how he keeps quiet. You should really call him and ask him yourself. He asks about you and your art. He says he never knows how you're doing."

"Sure," I said.

"We miss you," she said. "It'll be okay." But her voice was still laced with worry, and I couldn't keep talking to her, despite her kindness and love.

I hung up, crawled back into bed, and pulled the covers over my head.

Then I awoke to someone touching my face, poking it

repeatedly. My body jolted, my eyes shot open. It was the little men, gathered around me. They must have squeezed out from under the bathroom door. I was touched that their instinct was to find me, to be with me. I sat up slowly and they climbed into my lap. I put my hand over my crotch to keep them away from my morning wood. They looked up at me expectantly and made noises I couldn't interpret until my own stomach rumbled and I realized, Oh, they must be hungry.

So I made scrambled eggs with cheddar, pepper, and salt. I lifted the little men carefully, one by one, onto my kitchen table so they could eat with me. They were so small that what would have been a bite for me was enough to fill them. They tore apart the fluffy yellow egg with their hands and stuffed their faces. They were messy eaters, not caring if the juices and stray bits of food stuck to their naked bodies. I filled a blue bowl with water for them to drink from, but their peaceful drinking—cupping the water in their hands and bringing it to their greasy faces—did not last long. Once one jumped into the bowl, the rest did, too, splashing one another and making small puddles of water all over the table. I took several pictures with my phone of them playing. They were soaking wet and shrieking with joy and in a circle of blue on my black table. The late-morning light through the window made their skin glow warm. I sent the pictures to Seamus. He responded with three big heart-eyes emoji. *I love them!!!* he texted. When I finished eating, I dried each of them with my softest towel, and my hands were still shaking. Would they ever stop?

*   *   *

I will admit that I felt the little men were just as much Seamus's as they were mine, even then, when they were so new. Seamus was, after all, the one who had birthed them with me, wasn't he? We liked each other, very much so, but we weren't technically together. We were both too painfully aware of our age difference. All the time we spent together was predicated on the fact that we would fuck, which I loved, but sometimes I wanted more. Then the little men came. They were something special we shared. They were our children; we were their fathers. Their daddies.

Once, before the little men, Seamus had told me how much he disliked being called "Daddy." We were lying in his king-size bed, side by side. We'd just had sex. "Whenever I hook up with guys your age," he said, looking up at the ceiling, "they always want to call me Daddy. I'm fucking them and then they say some shit like 'Yes, Daddy,' or 'Oh, Daddy,' or 'I love your dick, Daddy,' and what am I supposed to say to that? *I love your ass, son. Open wider*? I mean, I get it. I just can't get into it. I want to fuck another *man*. I'm glad you're not like that."

"Oh, for sure," I said, looking up at the ceiling with him, as if I saw exactly what he saw up there, apart from the ceiling fan, even though I felt like I was just a child who could barely take care of himself and had the ridiculous impulse to make art, had no clue what he really wanted in life besides for as many people as possible to see his work, pay outrageous sums of money for it, and hail him as a great talent.

And the thing is, I would've called another man Daddy and I had called another man Daddy, on multiple occasions. I called them Daddy while catching my breath from sucking their cocks. I called them Daddy while they unlocked my ass with their tongues. I called them Daddy while they held me in their arms and kissed me on the cheek. When they said, "Take off your clothes, boy," I said, "Yessir." When they said, "Bend over, boy," I said, "Yessir." When they said, "Come for me, boy," I said, "Yessir." And on the rare occasion when they said, in a voice brusque and low, "I love you, son," I said, bright and earnest, "I love you too, Dad." The warmth in their eyes exposed something greater than pleasure, greater than desire. I was giving them something that stroked and soothed their souls.

I didn't look for these men, didn't seek out this particular fetish, but we found one another inevitably. My tastes in men ranged from younger to much older, and on the older end of the spectrum you were bound to find daddy-types, the ones who actually wanted to be called Daddy. But, really, a daddy could be any age, even younger than you. A daddy could be anyone. It was a name, a role. You could be anything as long as someone called you by it. I submitted to the fantasy and allowed it to bloom. *Daddy* was a spell that made men rough and gentle, demanding and giving. And the thing was, a son could always leave, a son was *expected* to leave someday and be his own man. A son didn't have to love his father the way a father had to love his son.

But to Seamus, as I lay warm and tired in bed with him, I was just another guy, another man. He loved the virility of my body, trim and hairy—though not as hairy as his. Just the right amount of fur, he often told me. This, too, I realized, was a role I played, the man he could both open up to and open up. I was always accepting the things men ascribed to me. I turned my gaze away from the ceiling and nuzzled my face into the crook of his shoulder, running my fingers through the hair on his chest, letting his burly arms wrap around me tighter, tighter.

After breakfast, I tied colored embroidery thread into loops for the little men to wear around their necks—not too tight, just loose enough for them to fit their heads through. I gave each one a different color—lapis, turquoise, chartreuse, peach, vermillion, and goldenrod—so I could tell them apart. It felt too soon to give them names, and what do you name that which was also you? The little men were taken with their necklaces at first, admiring the vibrant hues, putting the knots in their mouths to suck on. But soon they began to grab one another's threads, jerking one another's heads with each playful tug. I tried to stop them so they wouldn't strangle one another, but they darted around my bedroom floor too quickly for me to separate them without using force, and I feared hurting them.

To my relief, the threads came off their necks and were then twirled and thrown around, used for one-on-one games of tug-of-war. And then, just as soon as the play began, it stopped. They dropped the loops of thread, now bored of them. They realized they had the whole apartment to explore.

It wasn't a large apartment. I had only the furniture needed for a place to look furnished—armchairs, coffee table, desk, dresser—along with a number of art projects I'd accumulated over the years: cardboard boxes full of wheel-thrown bowls and mugs; a large cicada crudely tack-welded out of rusted rebar and sheet metal; a human-sized sculpture of a Barbie doll made of hot pink organza, pinned to the wall. As the little men scampered around, I rushed to hide all the dangerous things I could find—cleaning agents, knives, paint thinner, a splintering wood sculpture of a phallus impaled all over with nails—and put them out of reach, in closets and on top shelves. I kept a close eye on the little men and thought maybe I could identify them by the objects they were drawn to. This one seemed especially fascinated by the small bronze bust of Dolly Parton I used as a doorstop. This one stroked the soft white fur of my plump succulents perched by the window. This one climbed into a Cheetos bag I'd left on a chair and started coughing up the orange Cheetos dust.

But I soon found out that once one of the little men discovered something new, the others followed and joined in. They traveled as a pack and approached the world as a collective. They swarmed around an object, tasting it, feeling it, all its edges, all its surfaces, until one grew tired of it and branched out from the group in search of the next thing they would come to understand with their tiny hands and mouths.

It became clear that while they were as curious as toddlers, they were not quite as helpless or stupid. The world was new and strange to them and they wanted to know it all. But sometimes they proceeded with an undertone of caution, already knowing with an animal instinct that a cactus would prick them, or that a stray piece of glitter wasn't food to eat, or that fire would burn their skin when I lit a candle and put it on the floor to test them. They circled the flame and felt its warmth, marveling as it flickered and cast their shadows long behind them, but they didn't try to touch it. They kept their distance. And when they'd seen all they needed to see, they moved on.

It was in this way that I decided I could leave them alone in my apartment during the week when I went to work at the studio.

At the time, I was a resident "emerging artist" at a semi-notable ceramics studio, nearing the midpoint of my two-year stint there, and I had my first solo show coming up to commemorate it. The timing of the little men's appearance was not ideal. I'd spent the first ten months of my residency inviting men from Grindr to come to my studio and pose naked for me while I sculpted them. I would never mention sex, but under my intense gaze, as the facts of their flesh were translated into the wet, dark clay, they would all, without fail, become hard, and all the sculptures sported small, adamant erections. This was, in fact, how I'd met Seamus. He'd been the only one to insist that I get naked too. Well, that's not true. He was the only one who had convinced me.

So on Monday, I left the little men home alone with a bowl of food and a bowl of water in the kitchen and an empty bowl in the bathroom. Then I went to my studio and I lost myself to colors. The dried clay of my nude men ate up the peachy, umber, ocher, and beige underglazes as soon as I brushed them on. More and more I thought they were coming to life, and I was salivating. I could see it clearer and clearer: my show as a menagerie of men, a catalog of bodies that had yearned for my touch, a bold and provocative statement on queer male sexuality (a statement that, of course, I had yet to articulate). My biggest inspiration was Barbara King, a lesbian sculptor who gained prominence in the '70s for her stone carvings of vaginas that were so tender and exquisite that spirits came to nestle and live inside their folds, and I hoped my work could be as sensual and profound, would take on a life of its own. I loaded the sculptures into the kiln, careful not to bump and break their brittle bodies, and began firing them, very slowly. I hoped none of them would crack, warp, bloat, or explode.

When I came home, I found my apartment in shambles. Clothes, potting soil, and paper clips were strewn about the floor. Books and sketchbooks pulled from shelves and pages ripped out, ripped to pieces, confettied. Tubes of paint opened and squeezed out into puddles. Little footprints in phthalo blue, quinacridone magenta, and titanium white dotted the hardwood floor. I followed them to the closet, where I found the little men hiding in my shoes. They were covered in bright color and giggling, pleased to have been found. I shook them out of my sneakers and boots. "Go to the bathroom!" I yelled, and they grew quiet. Their faces wilted. They obeyed.

I scrubbed them clean. I wasn't gentle. The paint was, thankfully, acrylic, and peeled off their skin. "You can't make a mess like that," I scolded. "You live here, too, you know. I'm too tired to clean up after you." But I cleaned it all anyway. Their mess was my mess.

I made us orange rice and black beans for dinner. The beans looked like fruit in their hands as they ate quietly, ashamed, and it was so absurd, I couldn't help but laugh. The little men didn't understand what was funny, but they were happy to see me no longer angry, so they started laughing too. I took a picture of them, smiling and holding their giant beans, and sent it to Seamus.

Seamus responded: *Awwww!!*

And then: *Wanna come over? ;)*

Not tonight, I texted. *Tomorrow night?*

Sure! Bring the kiddos <3

And so on Tuesday I tried again. I told the little men, "You can play all you want, but don't make a mess. And if you do, you have to clean it up. Okay?" They nodded emphatically like good little boys. But they weren't little boys. They were me, a young man, only smaller. Their bodies were strong and hairy, their pubes dark and thick, and they shared my musk. When I came home that evening, things were as I'd left them, and the little men were asleep in my bed, snoring their little snores. And in their sleep, their little cocks were erect, too, pressing against their little hairy bellies. I wondered if they dreamed the same dream and if this dream was especially nice. I wondered, had they grown? I took out a ruler and found that, yes, they had: nearly an inch. I wondered if they would keep growing. I woke them. "We're going to see Papa," I joked, but they only looked at me, puzzled.

The little men loved climbing all over Seamus's hairy belly, holding on to his orange fur, pressing into his soft flesh as we lounged on his couch and watched TV. They tugged at his beard and blew raspberries into his armpits. Seamus giggled like a child. They cooed and purred at the sound of his gruff voice.

"They like me as much as you do!" he said.

No, I thought, they love you.

When Seamus and I wanted time alone, we put the little men in his spare bedroom and gave them markers and loose sheets of printer paper to play with. Then Seamus took me to his room and fucked me the way I love most to be fucked: lying flat on my belly as a man slides inside, his weight pressing me into the mattress, holding my body down. His face pressed into my neck, kissing that warm, pulsing stretch of muscle and flesh, grunting into my ear as I moan into the sheets and he thrusts inside me again and again, animal, deliberate, and I cannot go anywhere but to where he is pushing me—to pleasure, to fullness—till he bursts like a clam in a pan and I am more than pleased, more full than can be measured.

By the time we were done, we found that the little men had made the most wonderful lines and shapes across the papers and on their own little backs and bellies—scuttling, chasing, floating.

On Wednesday of that first week, I unloaded the kiln and was relieved to find all my nude sculptures were intact. I ignored a text from my father that said only *Hey mijo*.

On Thursday, I came home early and found the little men fucking.

I'd bought them a blueberry cake doughnut as a treat, a simple pleasure, but silly me for not thinking they would find pleasure themselves. There they were, in my bed, humping and yowling and kissing and more. Licking and sniffing their hairy little asses. Sucking and grasping their trembling little cocks. Biting and pinching their pink little nipples. Opening and scrunching their round, ruddy faces. All of which were, of course, my ass, my cock, my nipples, my face.

I couldn't look away.

Was that really how I looked when I fucked? The ugly O of my mouth, the spastic jerking of my hips, the strange squirming of my shoulders, the anxious twitching of my dick.

They didn't even notice I was there.

Could I blame them?

No.

But I couldn't help it. My lunch made its way up my throat and onto my floor.

The little men noticed only when my body hit the floor too.

I regained consciousness as the little men prodded my cheeks, their worried faces close to mine. They were now a good seven inches tall, and some of them were busy sopping up my vomit with a dirty dish towel, but they stopped and turned when I sat up. Relief smoothed their faces. One of them had fetched me a banana from my fruit bowl, which must've taken a great deal of effort. I put the banana aside and gathered them all to me and squeezed them tight against my chest till they squealed to be released.

I knew I shouldn't have been so upset about it: the little men were not children, were not *my* children—but they were. They were mine, my boys, and my discomfort persisted. I decided I couldn't leave them alone anymore. So Friday morning I put the little men in a picnic basket and carried them to work, where I could keep an eye on them all day. They loved the studio, all the knickknacks and clay tools to play with. "Don't stab him with the needle tool!" I warned one not five minutes after they crawled from the basket. The little man holding the needle tool like a spear pressed his palm against the metal point and, finding that it was indeed sharp, nodded solemnly. The rest had paid attention and I thought I'd prevented the worst from happening.

But soon they were climbing onto the table where my sculptures stood. The little men were now as tall as some of the sculptures, half as tall as others. "Be careful," I said, but they didn't hear me. They were entranced. The little men rubbed the clay figures' backs and chests, climbed on top of them, grabbed their dicks, licked the dry surfaces and found that the once-fired clay ate up the moisture. "*Careful*," I said again from across the room as I stirred a bucket of glaze, this time louder, sterner, and still they didn't acknowledge my command.

One of the little men found a sculpture sitting close to the edge. An eight-inch-tall rendering of a smooth and slender construction worker named Darius, wearing only his heavy work boots, standing with his arms crossed and his hips cocked to the side. The little man squeezed the sculpture's rigid flesh. I stopped my stirring, held my breath. To an untrained eye, the little man and the sculpture might have looked to be the same sort, made from the same mud and dirt, and perhaps you would think, for a moment, that the sculpture would suddenly come to life and twirl the little man in a slow dance. But what I saw was my failure. Next to the earnestness and energy of the little man's moving body, the sculpture appeared not just rigid but inarticulate, pathetic, bloodless, heartless. The torso, limbs, and face were frantically, hastily sculpted—smears and blocks of clay, rough and chalky, that merely approximated the shape of a man. It was only the penis, large compared to Darius's compact body, that held any life. How gently I'd bent the clay to capture its slight downward curve. How tenderly I'd smoothed and burnished it until it had its own sheen that invited you to touch it. How embarrassing to find I had sculpted a man's entire body only to get at his cock. How horrifying my failure was to me, so much so that I didn't even realize the sculpture was falling until it crashed to the floor.

The legs snapped off. The chest broke in two. A high crack sang through the studio.

Then a chorus of crashes followed as the other little men did as their brother did and took delight in the toppling. "Stop!" I cried, but my voice cracked and broke. The stiff bodies fell through space, and I watched it happen slowly, from afar, the breakage, limbs and heads skidding across the smooth concrete. The largest was a fifteen-inch-tall rendering of Seamus's burly body; it crashed like thunder, its belly bursting. The little men laughed and I started to cry.

It was not a slaughter but a mercy killing. How could I have been so foolish to think the work good and true and beautiful? The little men noticed my crying and stopped their carnage, but there was no way I could show the sculptures that were still intact to the rest of the world. I put the lid on the glaze bucket and stood. "Come on," I said to the little men. "We're going home."

As I drove, my sobs mounted, became ugly heaves and gulps of air. The little men watched me from the picnic basket, frightened by the convulsions distorting my face, which was theirs. I now had less than two months to come up with an entirely new show. The prospect felt, in that moment, impossible and devastating. Worse than the burning drip of chlamydia I'd caught from an unfaithful lover. Worse than any breakup with any of the boyfriends I'd thought I was sure to marry. Worse than the time my father called me a faggot for shying away from the hard arc of a soccer ball.

When I got home, I stripped off my clothes and crawled into bed, too exhausted to shake this morose weight. I ignored a text from Seamus, not even bothering to read it. All I wanted was to brood. All I wanted was to be alone.

But I wasn't alone. The little men climbed out of their picnic basket, into my bed, and onto my chest. They jumped up and down on me, yammering their gibberish, making silly faces, trying to cheer me up. I tried to smile for them, but it was a weak smile that only brought back my tears from earlier. They stopped their jumping and rushed to my face, no longer scared of my sadness. They kissed my cheeks and hugged my head and used their deft little fingers and smooth little palms to dry my tears. Swarmed by them, their bodies and hands pressing into my soft, supple skin, I felt my face taking on an expression of quiet joy, molded into a form that could hold their love.

It was clear to me what I should do. If the little men had pushed me over the edge and into this pit, they could help carry me out.

So I took them back to the studio that weekend and said, "Would y'all like to make art?" They cheered, throwing their arms up in the air, and I wanted to kiss them all. I did kiss them all. The next two months would be nothing but joyous work, exhausting work.

The *Happy Columns* series was my collaboration with the little men. I gave them each a column of clay as tall as they were and let them play. Eagerly, they raked their fingers through the soft and the grit; punched the solid surfaces over and over until they had cratered one side and made the mass lean over; bit off chunks and pressed those chunks back on to create a mound; hugged the clay and squeezed it with all the strength their little arms and legs could muster; pressed their faces in deep and left ghostly impressions. When they grew bored of the clay, having done all they wanted to do with it, I took each column, hollowed it out, and let it dry before painting it with underglaze—pops of baby blue, canary yellow, and carnation pink on the red-brown clay to emphasize the textures the little men had created. We did this every day for that first month and a half before the columns were fired and glazed, and every day they did something different to the clay, and every day the columns of clay I gave them got bigger and bigger because they got bigger too.

They were growing steadily. Ten inches, a foot, fourteen inches, sixteen, and more and more. I wondered how big they would get. They quickly outgrew the picnic basket, so I sewed them simple tunics out of lavender felt for them to wear when

I took them out. Of course, as soon as we got inside the studio, the little men would take the tunics off. They preferred to be naked. They liked the feeling of the clay pressed against their bare bodies.

People often stared at them, but there are stranger things in the world—ghosts slow-dancing in dive bars, firebirds nesting in backyard grills. And I was, strangely, not ashamed of them, as I'd thought I might be. I brought them along wherever I went, knowing they would always follow, which comforted me. Their company—the pitter-patter of their feet, their squeaking, wordless voices, their bodies close to mine— made me feel at ease and amazed by the world. I could explain the leaves of trees and bushes to them, describe the broad strokes of photosynthesis, and share in their wonder as they plucked a handful of leaves from a shrub, licked them, and pressed them to one another's faces like stickers.

Was this how my parents had felt about me when I was young, toddling after them in the grocery store or the art museum, asking endless questions, running out of sight? Was this how they had felt when I needed their warmth, when they held me?

In those two months, Seamus often came to the studio to bring me and the little men lunch during his breaks and dinner at night. "You need to eat more," he'd tell me, and he was right. I was forgetting to feed myself, I was so caught up in the work. "And you need to remember you're not just taking care of yourself anymore," he chastised me. "It may be okay if you go without a meal, but these little guys depend on you." He was more than right, and I was ashamed. "Will you help me?" I asked. "Of course," he said, and kissed me on the forehead.

Seamus would sometimes sit there in the studio and keep me company as I worked late into the night, even if he himself had worked a long, tiring day. I wasn't one for talking while working. I was sharply focused, my hands moving on their own, my mind tranced, but he didn't mind. He had the little men to care for and entertain, cutting chicken into chunks and pitting cherries for them to eat, rolling balls of clay across the floor for them to chase and smash. His voice was always gentle and made the little men calm. Often they napped on his chest and belly as he stretched out on a blanket, humming, dozing, telling them stories of his life.

I cherished this chance to get to know Seamus more deeply. He told us about his first blow job, from an unpopular kid at school; about his first love, his teammate on the football team, and the nights they'd spend in the woods; about his mother's obsession with avocado salads and his piece-of-shit father's devotion to the cowboy church in their hometown; about the woman he was almost engaged to at age twenty-two and how she'd even tried to make it work after he told her he was gay. He dipped down deep into the well of his past and I drank from the bucket in gulps.

Then one day, "I was married once," he said.

One of the little men was curled in his lap. They were now

an incredible eighteen inches tall. The others were covering themselves with slurry or they were off hiding in cabinets, kissing and fucking. They'd learned to do it where I couldn't see them, but we could still hear, and, for some reason, I didn't mind it much anymore.

"Oh," I said. "You never mentioned that."

So then he told me. How they had married up north, in a state where it was legal. How for five years they were happy. How they'd wanted children of their own, but down here, in the South, there were laws that made it difficult. And then there was his husband's addiction to gambling and amphetamines, which had come out of hiding like an ugly cat. There wasn't much Seamus could do. "By the time we were approved to adopt, it was too late: we were through." When gay marriage was legalized across the country, they were the first in the state to get divorced, having already been separated for years.

I stood up and stepped away from painting the columns. I went to him and rubbed his back, kissed his bald head. As he sat there before me, I pictured him as a father, so different from my own. His good humor, his soft touch, his ease in talking even about difficult things. "That's terrible," I said. "Is it too late?"

"It's over between us, Leo. I haven't seen him in years…"

"No," I said. "To adopt. To raise a child." The little man snored in Seamus's arms, his face serene. "You would be a wonderful dad."

You are a wonderful dad.

"I don't know, Leo." He wouldn't look at me. "I couldn't do it alone, not at this age."

And I wanted to say, *I would help you. I would.* But I didn't say it, because I didn't know if that was true, even as he was helping me. I only touched him more, as gently as I could, because that was all I knew.

The little man whimpered in his sleep. A nightmare was settling in.

A few years later I would be fucked in a sling by a sixty-year-old man, and he would ask me, "You like your daddy's dick, don't you?," and beneath the red light of his sex dungeon, having inhaled so many hits of poppers my lips were blue, I would say, "Yessir, I love it."

And then he would ask me, "You always wanted to be fucked by your dad, didn't you?," and in the moment, without thinking—the pressure, throb, and flesh of him inside me—I would say, "Yes, I did."

And then I would think, Oh, that's not true!

But then this daddy would take me down from his sling and lay me belly-down on the padded floor and press his body on top of mine, sliding his big dick into me, just the way I loved it, and I would remember one night when I was a child, when I couldn't sleep for fear of monsters. I woke my father and he followed me back to my room, where he crawled into my bed and slung his body on top of mine, the covers between us, his steady breath against my back and in my ear as he dozed. I had never felt so safe and secure in my small life, and I slept soundly. When the morning light woke me, my father was gone.

The day after Seamus opened up about his ex-husband, I called my mother.

"Leo!" she said. "Is everything all right?"

"Yes, yes," I said, nodding. "Everything's great! I just wanted to call."

The little men were putting on their felt clothes, babbling and milling about my knees. I was going to take them to the park, give them a break from the studio and let them roam free. They were looking a little pale and I figured they needed sun. The summer was fading, and with the coming change of seasons, the will-o'-the-wisps were starting to rise from their underwater sleep and float from swamp to forest to field. I thought the little men would like to chase their ethereal glow as the sun settled lower and lower in the sky.

"Well... how are they?" my mother asked nervously. She could hear them through the phone.

"They're so good, so wonderful," I said, looking down at them, their messy hair. They swayed, unsteady with their new height, as if it were a bit too much for them. "I can't wait for you to meet them."

At this she was silent, unsure of what to say. Something

heavy hung on the other end of the line. Then, finally, "Have you talked to your father recently?"

"No." I sighed. "He should call me if he wants to talk."

"He said he texted you. He said you didn't respond."

"That was weeks ago. I was busy and I've been exhausted." I made excuses. The little men were growing restless, licking and tugging on one another, driving one another nuts.

"I know, honey, but he's your father. He wants to talk to you."

"Then why doesn't he talk to me?" The little men began to shove one another.

"Why won't *you* talk to him, Leo?" Her voice was stern.

The little men then turned to me and started plucking out my leg hairs, stepping on my toes, biting my calves. "Ow! Stop that!"

"I can't keep being a carrier pigeon for you two," my mother said.

I glared down at the little men and stamped my feet. They scurried away.

"Just call him, *please*. He worries about you."

"Fine," I said, but I didn't mean it. For so long it had been this way, my father and I unable to really hear each other, as if one of us were under water. I wasn't ready to dive in or emerge; either would break the surface of something protecting me from the hard demands of love. A son shouldn't have to do that, I thought naively. "You're coming to my opening, right?"

"Of course, Leo," she said, her voice brightening. "We wouldn't dare miss it."

"So he's coming? Last time he came to an opening he called my work 'weird,' remember?"

"Honey, he brags about you all the time to his coworkers. He's very proud of you. We both are."

"Mmh," I said. I didn't believe it.

The little men were whining loudly at the door, their voices croaky, begging for tall grass, fresh air, and play. I said goodbye and hung up to answer their call and take them into the big, bright world.

In the weeks before the show, I spent my days unloading the happy columns from the kilns—their surfaces now glossy with clear glaze—and installing them in the gallery space. I painted the walls a deep forest green that nestled the warm pop of the red clay, and I placed the columns, clustered like groups of partyers or alone like prima ballerinas, on low pedestals so the little men could see them and everyone else would have to crouch to look closely. I was more than pleased; I was ecstatic about how everything was coming together. The columns danced, radiating like plants in bloom, moaning their obscene shapes to attract insects and make seed. They were phallic, yes, but they were more than that. They were living creatures, bending, twisting, stretching; touched tenderly and violently, caressed and clawed; and it was the scars from these touches that made them alive, that gave them blood. It was the first time I saw what my hands—what the little men's hands—were truly capable of. I knew even then that my work would never be the same.

So to show the little men my unending thanks, I spent my nights that week sewing dapper pink capes and mint green shorts for them to wear to the reception. Though they preferred being naked, they eagerly eyed their new clothing and begged me to let them wear it, pawing at the soft silk. "Not today," I said. "You have to wait till the opening, when everyone will see all the wonderful, beautiful work we've made." They nodded big in agreement.

But then, two mornings before the opening, as I woke throbbing for the new day, the little men didn't rise as eagerly as I did. "Get up, you lazy bums!" I said, and three of the little men rose from the nest of blankets and pillows they'd made on the floor beside my bed, but slowly and wearily. Two others knelt beside one who seemed to still be asleep, so quiet, peaceful. The little men were now nearing a full two feet tall, but they were unable to stay balanced and kept falling to their knees. I knelt on the floor. "Is everything okay?" I asked, and they said nothing. I nudged the sleeping little man and found he was not sleeping. His body rolled over limply.

"Wake up," I said, as if this would bring him back to life.

I picked him up and held him to my chest. My heart beat so slow and so hard I thought maybe he could hear it like a rousing bass drum, but this, too, proved utterly useless. There was no more warmth in his body. There was no more quick little pulse. I looked at the others. Their skin was so pale, the blue of their veins showing, and they were breathing heavily, as if each breath were an attempt to hold on to something that only slipped through.

"Not you too," I said, and one by one, over the next hour, they started to collapse.

I could do nothing but catch them as they fell. Do nothing but pull the rest of them close before they fell, too, and wait for them all to die. They were not sad or anxious or sobbing helplessly, as I was. They only seemed tired—terribly exhausted—as if they had spent all the energy, awe, and love they'd been allotted and now it was time to go.

And this, I realized, was why my relatives had abandoned their little men in the jungle. Not because of the burden of care they required but the burden of loss they promised, and so soon.

I lay on the floor all morning, holding the six of them to my bare chest, keeping my eyes closed, waiting to die too.

But, of course, I didn't die, as much as it pained me. And as much as it pained me, eventually I had to sit up and then stand, lifting their weight with me. I'd never felt so weak. I laid them down on my bed in a row and covered them with the sheet. I didn't want to look at their lifeless faces and their lifeless bodies, which were my lifeless face and my lifeless body.

I needed help. I needed not to be alone.

I called Seamus but his phone rang and rang and he didn't answer. Maybe he was busy at work. Or maybe he was ignoring my calls. Were we already, by then, starting to slip apart? So I called my mother. Her phone rang and rang as well, but eventually she picked up.

"Mom?" I barely managed, stifling sobs.

A low, clear voice that was not my mother's answered. "Leo?" it said.

"Dad?" I sniveled. "Where's Mom?"

"She's out shopping. She left her phone at home: you know how she is, that woman. What—what happened? Mijo? Did they...? Are you...?"

I didn't know how to answer him, other than to say, "They're gone, they're gone." I didn't know how to explain the pain; it was as total and all-consuming as the joy the little men had made me feel. "They're gone," I said once more. And then I cried and cried over the phone, saying no words, choking on loss, hoping it was somehow a language my father could understand.

WILD HONEY HAS A SCENT OF FREEDOM
by ANNA AKHMATOVA

Translated by Katie Farris and Ilya Kaminsky

Wild honey has a scent—of freedom.
Dust—a scent of sunshine.
And a girl's mouth—of violets.

But gold—nothing.
Water—like mignonette.
And, like apple—love.
But we have learned that

Blood smells only of blood.

(1934)

THE SORROWS
OF OTHERS

by ADA ZHANG

THE APARTMENT WAS EERILY clean, and he wondered if she had not been trying to restore the place so much as to make it foreign to him. Surfaces shone. Fruit, which he always let sit in plastic bags, now rested decoratively in a glass bowl. Even useless objects in drawers, trinkets and receipts that had somehow accumulated, were given their own containers, shallow jewelry boxes she had presumably collected over the years and brought with her to her new home. She had been there for only one night, and already he had to ask her, his new wife, where to find his lightweight coat, his materials for calligraphy, the small spoons he liked for his tea.

"You sit," she said to him, getting up from the couch where she was reading a newspaper. He saw when she put it down that it was one from last month. "I'll get it."

Before he could object and say that the tea had already been made, that he just needed to know where the spoons were, she was off. Her steps were small, he noticed, and quick, slippers clapping evenly from the living room all the way to the kitchen.

When his daughter called a month earlier to say she had found the perfect match—someone he might connect with, since the woman happened to be from his hometown—his reaction had moved from shock to humiliation. He had no idea that his daughter had been searching, or that his current situation was a problem that needed to be resolved.

"I'm fine on my own," he'd said to Xiao An, following a silence on the phone.

"She's never been married," she replied. "In her forties. Parents dead. No kids. Also, you're both from Changwu, so you'll already have something to talk about. I'm telling you, Ba, even fate couldn't have come up with someone better."

"I don't understand. How did this come about?"

"A matchmaking agency called Planet Love, for people middle-aged and older. I made you a profile. Ba, don't be prudish," Xiao An continued when he was quiet. "Everyone goes through a matchmaker these days. The young, the rich. Everyone's looking for love."

His daughter, whom he affectionately called Little

Comfort, had been motherless since she was two years old. She possessed a determination that she had gotten from neither him nor her mother, and every time she sensed an opportunity, she was quick to snatch it up. She had moved to Shanghai for college and had been there ever since. Twice a year she came back to Xi'an to check on her father, and to complain to him about the rigors of life in a Tier One city: the housing market, construction, supermodels and actors walking with their noses up, as though the whole city stank, which, she added, it did. She compared it with the relative ease of Xi'an, which was still considered Tier Two, though they both knew that with tourism on the rise all over the country, the imperial capital was also changing.

Songhao had a humbler attitude toward risk, harboring the superstition that only if he rarely took chances would the world occasionally give him what he wanted. His first marriage to the woman he loved was his prize, he'd thought, for living cautiously, until one day his young wife died of an aneurysm in her sleep. After that he stopped believing in this formula, but his aversion to risk grew harsher. He stared at his dead wife's photograph once a month, keeping it in the drawer of his nightstand where he also stored the watch she'd given him on his twenty-sixth birthday, at the beginning of their love, which ended up being not far from the end.

His sole ambition now was to live a quiet life, not to disturb others or be disturbed. He'd remained single for the past thirty-two years. Another person could only bring complications.

"What does she want out of marriage?" Songhao asked his daughter. "Does it say anywhere in her profile?"

"It says she wants a roommate to whom she can offer her sympathy," Xiao An said. "Not exactly the most exciting plea for romance, but it looks like that's all she put."

"I've rearranged, I think you've noticed," Yulan called from inside the kitchen, as though having read his mind. Without thinking, Songhao had taken her place in the center of the couch. Realizing he was sitting in her warmth, he scooted over hastily. "You'll tell me," she said, "if I've gone too far."

She emerged with the tea on a tray and sat across from him, on the other side of the coffee table. He watched as she poured the tea confidently, as though this had been her apartment all along and he were just visiting.

"Not to worry," he said. "The mess was fine for a bachelor, but not suitable for two. Everything is much better." He picked up his cup to hide his face, embarrassed at his readiness to please, a quality he'd always despised in himself.

"Wait," she said. "Have some honey."

He liked his tea bitter, he was going to say, but was too slow. She had already opened a small jar next to the teapot and was dipping a generous serving into his cup, using one of those little spoons that he liked and that he still did not know where to find. She stirred until the amber had dissolved, and the spoon— she tapped it twice, on the edge of his cup—came out clean.

"Honey has a lot of healing properties." She set the spoon down on the tray. "It's good for digestion and regulating body temperature. We need those things as we get older."

He would have found her irritating were he not impressed by how in control she appeared in her new setting. Her movements were swift yet not at all hurried. Her profile on Planet Love revealed that before this, she'd been living with her sister in a traditional home with three rooms, a kitchen, and a small court-yard in the center. The information was on the third page of her profile, behind facts about hair color, face shape, face pigment, shoe size. It had comforted him that he could picture how she lived, since the home he'd grown up in had been similar. He and Yulan were both from Changwu, that was true, but his daughter had overlooked the more compelling coincidence that they were also both from Yaertou, a compound within the village. It was this detail, discovered on their first and only meeting, that had brought his old superstition back. He'd agreed to the marriage wondering if it wasn't fate at work after all.

The café where they had met was dark. Yulan happened to be in the city visiting a nephew and had reached out to Xiao An the night before. They might never have met otherwise.

"People leave home seeking change," she had said, when he'd asked why she never left Yaertou. "But to me, home is where you experience the most change, should life bid you stay. People go, new people come. Buildings are demolished and rebuilt, or abandoned. Children grow up. The truest change, the kind that changes you, happens when you don't choose it."

The fact that she was choosing to leave Yaertou now was not lost on him, but he didn't ask further questions. He hadn't been back there since his parents passed, but as if it were an etching in his mind, he could picture the four-hour bus ride that Yulan had taken to get to Xi'an, having made the trip many times when he was in college. The apple trees, then cornfields, then wheat fields, the world opening wide like a mouth before being siphoned into the throat of skyscrapers, smog, traffic, advertisements, the city. Yesterday they had met in the office of civil affairs. They were married in under ten minutes and afterward took a taxi back to his apartment, where Yulan got straight to tidying up, refusing the cantaloupe he sliced as well as his offer to take her out to dinner. It wasn't late, but she told him to get some rest, as though he were the one who'd made the long journey.

"You know, before you, I hadn't met another person from Changwu, let alone Yaertou, in many years," he said now. "Funny, isn't it? How we never know when our past and present might meet."

She smiled, revealing one crooked gray tooth on the top left. She wasn't bad-looking, he decided. There was a girlishness in her round face, and she was neither thin nor fat, just sturdy, a body that paired well with her manner.

"It is strange," she said. "What might be even stranger is that I have memories of you, from when you used to come back. I was a girl. I doubt if you would remember me."

He was jolted by this framing of their seventeen-year age

difference. He was sixty-one; she was forty-four. If they had married years ago, when she was in her twenties, they might have raised eyebrows, spurred judgments, but now no one would even look twice at them on the street. His wife was younger, but not young, and he was old. They were both past the age when people worried about their potential losses.

"Drink your tea," she said. "Don't let it get cold."

He took one long sip, then another.

"I know that your first wife passed away unexpectedly. You labeled yourself a widower on Planet Love, but I remember you from when you were married. Your wife was gorgeous, and so modern. I was twelve when the news got around…"

She spoke faster.

"People talked about it because you were sort of a big deal, one of the first from Yaertou to be admitted to a university. My mother always told me that if I studied hard, I could be like that Uncle who lived in Xi'an, I could get out of the village and live in the big city. It was a long time ago, but I think it's only respectful that I offer my belated condolences."

Something about the way she said the last part—with her head down, occasionally flicking her eyes up at him—felt like an invitation. It was his fault he hadn't prepared for this. Privacy wasn't prized where he and Yulan were from, a community comprising only ninety families. He'd gotten too comfortable in his solitude, protected by the anonymity of sharing a city with over twelve million others.

"It was a long time ago," he said, "but now that we're talking about it, I remember you too."

It was a lie. He had no memory of her at all, had trouble even conceiving of her as a child, but the least he could do was try to match her sense of their familiarity. He kept on lying. "Your face hasn't really changed."

Her gray tooth showed again. "A lot of people tell me that."

"What is Changwu like these days? It's bigger now, I imagine."

"In the countryside it's mostly seniors. Young people either live in the township or have moved away. My favorite of my sister's children just moved to Shenzhen for college. Your daughter lives in Shanghai, right? What does she do?"

"She manages musicians at a record label."

He repeated some jargon that Xiao An had thrown at him over the years, but the truth was he wasn't exactly sure what his daughter did. She traveled a lot and was always too busy to provide a proper explanation. But Yulan seemed satisfied. She nodded with her mouth open, and he felt relieved that they had moved into more pragmatic territory. It seemed like they were hitting a stride.

"Do you like the tea?" Yulan asked. "How is it with honey?"

"Good," he lied again. "Good."

* * *

He woke up from his afternoon nap to find his books in the living room newly shelved next to the television. The glass case, which held Xiao An's old toys and some souvenirs, had been dusted and wiped down. It caught the glare from the sun. The items now sat gingerly against a backdrop of spines, angled so they complemented one another.

The colorful and intentional display gave an upbeat quality to the room. He felt only slightly exasperated that he'd gotten used to his scattered stacks, that he could point to any surface and say what book used to be there, having created a system out of his disorderliness. He'd long ago memorized where in the apartment the floors creaked, what type of clicking came from the radiator versus from the walls compressing and stretching at night. But seeing how different everything was, he felt suspicious that his home, now, would betray him.

To make sure he was alone, he called out Yulan's name.

No one answered.

"Yulan?" he called again.

Back in his room, he shut the door silently and phoned Xiao An. She answered on the first ring, but it was loud where she was; they had trouble hearing each other. He tried speaking again once it got quiet but became seized by a cough. He sat down on the bed. Xiao An asked if he was okay, her concern sounding too close to pity.

He'd called to tell her about the spoons. They'd been a gift from Xiao An a few years ago, a six-piece set she'd brought back from London. Instead, he asked what she was up to.

"We took some clients out to lunch. The restaurant is packed. I'm in the bathroom."

"I've bothered you at work."

"It's not a big deal."

"Next time don't pick up."

"When did you become so considerate? Is everything okay? You didn't knock your head, did you?"

This was closer to their normal rapport, but the pity was still detectable. Why else had he called, if not to receive pity? Yulan had done nothing wrong, yet here he was acting like a child, ready to tattle on his wife to his daughter.

"Everything's great," he said. "Yulan has been reorganizing. She's completely transformed the place."

"Good. It desperately needed a makeover."

"What if I can't do this, Xiao An?"

"Do what?"

"What if I'm too used to being alone?"

He knew it was because his daughter loved him that she had signed him up for Planet Love, because she loved him that she had sifted through so many women's profiles, looking for someone who could cook and clean and who might need a man just enough to find a retired chemist attractive but not enough to exploit his modest government stipend. Marrying Yulan was his way of accepting his daughter's love, but he hadn't considered the practical benefit for Xiao An, how it would only become greater as he aged. Every time she came home, she teased him about some new habit he'd picked up, walking around with glasses perched on his head or, the latest, pitching his entire torso forward to sit. But it was true, his eyesight was getting worse. One day he might need the anchor of another person to help lower him down.

"I don't want to be someone's burden," he said, not sure whom he was talking about anymore.

"You raised me by yourself." Her words came with a small echo. "Was I a burden to you?"

"That's different," he replied.

"How so?"

What had happened to Xiao An to give her such a functional view of companionship? She'd had boyfriends before, but none of them was ever serious enough, she'd said, to be worthy of an introduction. Maybe he would have taken her mother for granted had she lived longer, had his feelings for her had time to wane and grow, eventually taking a familial shape. He still loved her for who she was when she died, someone separate from him and therefore incomprehensible to him. It was a wonder that she'd been with him at all.

When Xiao An was growing up, other parents had attributed her precociousness to being motherless, saying that it had made her perceptive and sweet, but Songhao didn't like how that discredited his daughter's natural abilities, meanwhile implying that goodness came from tragedy. Goodness came from goodness, he'd tried to teach Xiao An, by giving her the most carefree childhood he could imagine. The two of them fed ducks at the park every weekend until she was eighteen, a tradition they reprised now and then, passing a stick of candied hawthorn between them by the water. But she was an adult now. She should have the kind of love he'd had, even knowing how things had ended.

He felt hopeful for Xiao An, which made him happy. As with any true happiness, grief was there along the edges. His daughter should be open to love, young love, but that required being open to pain.

"You should get back to your party," he said to her.

"I have a few minutes."

"There are errands I need to run."

"Liar."

He could tell she was smiling.

"Fine," she said. "But let's pick a date for me to visit soon. Give Yulan ahyi my best and tell her I look forward to meeting her."

He waited for her to hang up, but Xiao An didn't end the call. He sat there listening to the sounds of the restaurant, picturing his daughter in her life, until he heard footsteps at the front door.

As the weeks went by, Songhao observed Yulan rearranging his schedule just as she had done with his things. On his own, he'd come to depend on his routine, the way it salved the daily task of passing time, but with Yulan the days passed quickly and without much effort, so while it was unsettling at first when she suggested doing something new, after a while he didn't mind following the trail of another person's decision-making. Calligraphy moved to before bed so they could take a walk together in the morning. His tea was shifted to noon. On Tuesdays and Thursdays, their walks were combined with tennis racquet aerobics in the park, an activity they picked up by chance one morning after a woman offered to let Yulan borrow her racket. Yulan turned out to be excellent; she was also younger than everyone in the group by at least ten years. She stood at the edge and completed the motions with a forcefulness that made it look like she was playing real tennis, slices and backhands at an invisible ball, while the rest of them, including him, looked as if they were square dancing with paddles.

Yulan took Xiao An's old room while Songhao continued sleeping in the bed he'd shared with his first wife. It was the only place in the apartment that was still his, that Yulan had not touched. At first this comforted him, but soon it made him uneasy, and he would hold off going to his room until he was on the very cusp of sleep, nodding off while brushing his teeth. Sex was never a question. He'd been grateful and horrified, upon reviewing his own Planet Love profile, to see that Xiao An had checked "Not interested" for him. Yulan had checked the same. He was curious whether his daughter viewed him as inherently sexless, but had neither the courage nor the indecency to ask.

By week seven, spring had turned to summer, and they had firmly established their places in the home. After lunch, he stayed at the table reading a book while Yulan sat cross-legged on the couch with her newspaper. It was never the paper of the day but an old issue, as though it took a month or two for the news of the world to ripen into Yulan's own personal tragedy. A talented young biochemist poisoned by jealous peers; a stabbing on a train; a woman who stomped a kitten to death in high heels, in a video that had gone viral. Yulan expressed these miseries to him every day over dinner, as they sat facing each other at the table that separated the living room from the entrance.

"Another building collapsed," she said to him one night, holding her bowl and chopsticks limply, as though in presentation. "In Wenzhou. Twenty-two people died. Did you know?"

The news had made international headlines weeks ago, cited as the deadliest case of building collapse that the country had seen in recent years, ever since these ramshackle tofu houses started popping up all along city perimeters, providing shelter for migrant workers.

"I had no idea," he said, keeping his gaze low. "What happened?"

"There were four buildings. They were put up quickly, and no one enforced construction codes. The buildings collapsed at three in the morning. Can you imagine? One second, you're getting a glass of water or going to the bathroom, thinking you're at home, you're safe. The next second, the ceiling falls, the ground slips away, and you're dead."

He imagined the scenario as Yulan described it but would never have if it hadn't been for her insistence. He did not possess her ability to see the likelihoods of other people's lives.

"A three-year-old survived the crash," she said. "Her father shielded her from the impact. He was one of the twenty-two who were found dead."

Her head had sunk between her shoulders. She hadn't touched her food. He couldn't understand what it was like to feel this deeply for strangers, but he supposed this was a way to stay afloat on top of loneliness, buoyed by the sorrows of others. He thought maybe that was how she'd remained on her own for so long, and why she had picked him out of all the bachelors on Planet Love, because only a longtime widower could understand her propensity to sadness.

"You should eat," he said, and pinched a bundle of mustard greens into her bowl.

"I'm not hungry," she replied.

A few times since moving in, Yulan had casually brought up his first wife, always flicking her eyes up at him like she had that first morning. While he knew that, as a couple, they should be able to talk about their pasts, he was feeling more and more like he didn't want to. He wished to keep his heartbreak close, not let it enter the torrent of all the world's misfortunes, which were infinite, as Yulan had proved over the weeks, no one more special than the rest.

She set her bowl down and moved to the couch.

"I can bring the food over to you," he said from the table. "If you would like."

"No, that's all right. You go on and eat."

She grabbed a newspaper from the coffee table shelf, an

issue so old and worn that when she opened it, it didn't make a sound.

Something caught his eye. Above Yulan's head, next to the south-facing window, was a group of framed photographs that had always been there, of him and his daughter at various moments in her childhood—birthdays, graduations, the zoo— but now there was a new picture, hanging on its own above the others. His glasses weren't nearby. He squinted to see the photograph of his first wife, the one from his bedside drawer.

Yulan had gone into his room. When?

How many times had he stared at that photo? Hundreds, probably. Her eyes, as bright and as unassuming as they'd been on the day she and he first met, when they were students at the university. The photo captured the thoughtless smile of someone for whom death felt so far away, it was basically impossible. Songhao blinked. Beneath his first wife, Yulan's head moved back and forth as she scanned the page, searching for another story.

Yulan couldn't take away his sorrow, but in living with her, he thought perhaps there was a place for it. His sadness and privacy complemented her sadness and openness, and in that way, each person had nothing to hide. They could be themselves.

Songhao turned back to his food and reached in. The pork and vegetables were delicious. Tomorrow, he decided, he would go to the newsstand and buy as many newspapers as he could carry home in his arms, current editions and back issues. If anyone asked, he would say they were a gift for his wife.

ANNA AKHMATOVA is one of Russia's most beloved poets. Born in 1889 in Odessa, she is particularly well known for her lyric poetry, which ranges from chronicles of Stalin's terror, to love lyrics, to elegies for poets of her generation. Her works have reached millions of readers all over the world.

T. C. BOYLE's "Dog Lab," along with a previous *McSweeney's* story, "The Apartment," will be part of the author's thirtieth book of fiction, a collection of thirteen new stories called *I Walk between the Raindrops*, which is scheduled for release this year. His most recent novel, published in September of 2021, is *Talk to Me*, and he is currently at work on *Blue Skies*, a novel focusing on climate change, invasive species, and extinction—joyous topics all. It is not a sequel to 2000's *A Friend of the Earth*, but employs that novel's method of projecting into the near future in order to assess what is happening in the present to us poor, benighted human animals.

SHAYNA CONDE is a New Jersey–based writer born to a Jamaican Virgo and a Haitian Pisces (and, yes, she is accepting thoughts and prayers). She spends her free time watching anything narrated by David Attenborough, aggressively avoiding sales at DSW, and writing about Black representation in entertainment on her Substack, "Heart to Arts." Shayna's poetry collection was a semifinalist for the 2021 Cave Canem Poetry Prize, and she is working on an essay collection.

HERNAN DIAZ is the author of two novels that have been translated into more than twenty languages: *In the Distance*, a finalist for the Pulitzer Prize and the PEN/Faulkner Award, and *Trust*, forthcoming from Riverhead Books in May 2022. His work has been published in the *Paris Review*, *Granta*, *Playboy*, the *Yale Review*, and elsewhere.

KATIE FARRIS is the author of the forthcoming poetry collection *Standing in the Forest of Being Alive* (Alice James Books, 2023). Her work appears in the *Nation*, *Poetry*, *American Poetry Review*, and elsewhere. Her chapbook, *A Net to Catch My Body in Its Weaving*, recently won the Chad Walsh Poetry Prize from *Beloit Poetry Journal*.

KATE FOLK's fiction has appeared in the *New Yorker*, *Granta*, *Zyzzyva*, and elsewhere. Her story collection, *Out There*, will be published in 2022 by Random House. She lives in San Francisco.

TEDDY GOLDENBERG is an Israeli cartoonist, artist, and landscape architect. Born in 1985, he began creating comics in 2003. His stories usually combine horror with humor. His work is featured in the new anthology *The Graphic Canon of Crime and Mystery, Vol. 2*; he recently created a two-part unauthorized graphic sequel to the 1985 American action film *Cobra*, which he named *Cobra II*; and his book *City Crime Comics* will be released in 2022.

NICKY GONZALEZ's short stories have appeared in *Kenyon Review* online, the *Massachusetts Review*, and *Taco Bell Quarterly*. They are working on a horror novel and a collection of stories set in South Florida. She has received support from Millay Arts, the Hambidge Center, and the Granum Foundation.

SAMANTHA HUNT's letter concerning the ghosts in our machines will be published in April 2022 in *The Unwritten Book*.

Hunt's nonfiction collection includes a number of essays on things that haunt: dead people, the forest, motherhood, hoarding, booze, the library of books we'll never have time to read or write. Nestled within *The Unwritten Book* is an incomplete manuscript about people who can fly without wings, written by Hunt's dad and found in his desk just days after he died.

ILYA KAMINSKY is the author of *Deaf Republic* (Graywolf Press) and *Dancing in Odessa* (Tupelo Press) and the coeditor of *Ecco Anthology of International Poetry* (HarperCollins).

STEPHEN KING is the author of more than sixty books, all of them worldwide best sellers. His recent work includes *Billy Summers*, *If It Bleeds*, and *The Institute*. King is the recipient of the 2018 PEN America Literary Service Award, a 2014 National Medal of Arts, and the 2003 National Book Foundation Medal for Distinguished Contribution to American Letters. He lives in Bangor, Maine, with his wife, novelist Tabitha King.

TAISIA KITAISKAIA is the author of four books: *The Nightgown and Other Poems*; *Literary Witches: A Celebration of Magical Women Writers*, a collaboration with artist Katy Horan and an NPR Best Book of 2017; and *Ask Baba Yaga: Otherworldly Advice for Everyday Troubles*, as well as its follow-up, *Poetic Remedies for Troubled Times: From Ask Baba Yaga*. Her work has appeared in journals such as *A Public Space*, *American Short Fiction*, the *Los Angeles Review of Books*, *Black Warrior Review*, and *Guernica*. She is the recipient of fellowships from the Michener Center for Writers and the Corporation of Yaddo.

AFABWAJE KURIAN is a graduate of the Iowa Writers' Workshop and is currently at work on her debut novel.

CARL NAPOLITANO is a writer, ceramicist, and drag performer
from Little Rock, Arkansas. He is a graduate of the Iowa Writers'
Workshop, and his work has appeared in the *Rumpus*, *Oxford
American*, and elsewhere. You can follow him on Instagram at
@carlnap.

VICTOR LADIS SCHULTZ lives near Chicago. His short stories
have appeared or are forthcoming in various publications, including *Chicago Quarterly Review*, *Ruminate*, and *Chiricú Journal:
Latina/o Literatures, Arts, and Cultures*. He is a proofreader for
Constelación, a bilingual magazine of speculative fiction.

CORINNA VALLIANATOS is the author of a novel, *The
Beforeland*, and a story collection, *My Escapee*. Stories from her new
collection have appeared or are forthcoming in *LitMag*, *Story*, and
Prairie Schooner. She lives in California.

ADA ZHANG is a graduate of the Iowa Writers' Workshop. Her
debut collection of stories, *The Sorrows of Others*, will be published
by A Public Space Books in spring 2023.

McSWEENEY'S 64: THE AUDIO ISSUE

Combining art, fiction, audio, and over a dozen unclassifiable print objects in a custom box, *McSweeney's 64* is a riotous exploration of audiovisual storytelling, coproduced with Radiotopia from PRX. Included are Rion Amilcar Scott, with a short fiction piece featuring two alternative audio endings; Pulitzer Prize–nominated composer Kate Soper, with a transhumanist, interactive software upload; Deaf-Blind poet John Lee Clark on the limits of accessibility; Aliya Pabani, with a radio drama whose plot is complicated by a 24" × 30" illustrated poster; Ian Chillag, with an absurdist, interactive phone tree; James T. Green, Catherine Lacey, and *This American Life*'s Sean Cole, with voicemail dispatches to the editor; Kali Fajardo-Anstine, Aimee Bender, and Kelli Jo Ford, with short stories that braid in audio; and so much more.

ALSO AVAILABLE
FROM McSWEENEY'S

FICTION

ART AND COMICS

BOOKS FOR CHILDREN

NONFICTION

HUMOR

POETRY

COLLINS LIBRARY

ALL THIS AND MORE AT

store.mcsweeneys.net

Founded in 1998, McSweeney's is an independent publisher based in San Francisco. McSweeney's exists to champion ambitious and inspired new writing, and to challenge conventional expectations about where it's found, how it looks, and who participates. We're here to discover things we love, help them find their most resplendent form, and place them into the hands of curious, engaged readers.

THERE ARE SEVERAL WAYS TO SUPPORT MCSWEENEY'S:

Support Us on Patreon
visit *www.patreon.com/mcsweeneysinternettendency*

Subscribe & Shop
visit *store.mcsweeneys.net*

Volunteer & Intern
email *eric@mcsweeneys.net*

Sponsor Books & *Quarterlies*
email *amanda@mcsweeneys.net*

To learn more, please visit *www.mcsweeneys.net/donate*
or contact Executive Director Amanda Uhle at
amanda@mcsweeneys.net or 415.642.5609.

McSweeney's Literary Arts Fund is a nonprofit
organization as described by IRS 501(c)(3).
Your support is invaluable to us.